The MG Collection

Patrick Stephens Limited, an imprint of Haynes Publishing, has published authoritative, quality books for enthusiasts for more than a quarter of a century. During that time the company has established a reputation as one of the world's leading publishers of books on aviation, maritime, military, model-making, motor cycling, motoring, motor racing, railway and railway modelling subjects. Readers or authors with suggestions for books they would like to see published are invited to write to: The Editorial Director, Patrick Stephens Limited, Sparkford, Nr Yeovil, Somerset, BA22 7JJ.

The MG Collection

THE POST-WAR MODELS

RICHARD MONK
Foreword by Roche Bentley

Patrick Stephens Limited

First published 1995 by Patrick Stephens Limited
in association with the MG Owners' Club.

Reprinted 1996 and 1997

The MG badge and octagon are registered
trade marks and are used by kind permission
of the Rover Group.

British Library Cataloguing-in-Publication Data:
A catalogue record for this book
is available from the British Library

ISBN 1 85260 516 2

Patrick Stephens Limited is an imprint of
Haynes Publishing, Sparkford,
Nr Yeovil, Somerset, BA22 7JJ

Tel. 01963 440635 - Fax 01963 440001
Int. tel. +44 1963 440635 - Fax +44 1963 440001

E-mail: sales@haynes-manuals.co.uk
Web site: http:/www.haynes.com

Designed and typeset by Kelvin Blyth Studios, Swavesey, Cambridge.
Printed in Italy by G. Canale & C. S.p.A. - Borgaro T.se - TURIN

Contents

Foreword

The luckiest people in the world are those who are able to combine their careers with their hobbies. Richard Monk and I are two such people and even after 21 years, the enthusiasm and our affection for the marque has not waned, nor is it ever likely to do so.

I first met Richard Monk at one of the very early Club events. It was at Pulloxhill, near Luton and when Richard and his wife arrived in their MGB GT, I was breathless trying to organise all manner of things, and to cap it all there were complaints about the overflowing loos! Richard could see a bad situation developing and offered his help. I politely declined as he had just paid to come in and was expecting an enjoyable day out. Another complaint arrived about the state of the loos and I jumped at Richard's offer! No, I didn't send him to fix the loos, it was me who pulled the short straw! By the time I had returned, Richard had sorted the judges for the concours, got the driving tests underway, arranged volunteers to help with the parking and fixed the PA system; I could see that he would be a tremendous asset to the Club.

Richard was working for British Telecom at the time, on the maintenance of telephone exchanges. Within a short space of time, he and I discussed the possibilities of full time employment with the Club. Basically I made him an offer he could not refuse. No job security, less money, long hours and working most weekends! He hesitated for a split second and then accepted. Over the years, as the Club grew Richard found himself becoming an expert on many varied tasks such as transferring the Club records from an antiquated manual system on to computer, answering technical queries from members and so on. He now manages the MGOC from our purpose-built headquarters in Swavesey ensuring that members continue to receive a first class service on all their MG requirements.

So now we come to *The MG Collection*. Richard being a first class photographer (another one of his hobbies), with the experience of many weddings involving fussy mums-in-law and argumentative relatives, thought MGs would make more appealing subjects. In producing material for the Club's magazine, *Enjoying MG*, he has built up a tremendous library of photographs from 'Old Number One' to the present day MGF sports car. His detailed close up shots and easily readable technical descriptions have enabled everyone to appreciate and understand the beauty of the many different MGs which have been built over the last 70 years. In the first volume of Richard's work we had the most marvellous pictorial coverage of the pre-war MGs. In this, the second volume, we have the post-war models; MGs which are more familiar to us, yet we learn so much from Richard's photographs and descriptions. I do hope that you enjoy the two volumes of *The MG Collection* as much as I do. For me they sum up the glorious history of the marque and are definitive publications for all MG enthusiasts.

Roche Bentley
Club Secretary
MG Owners' Club

TC Midget

The MG TC Midget is probably one of the best known MGs to come out of Abingdon since the Second World War. As soon as the war was over the factory resumed car production after six years of producing tanks, armoured cars and aeroplane engines for the war effort. The basis of the new car was the pre-war MG TB, it was to have a similar engine and gearbox and axles, the only significant changes would be to the body which was widened by nearly 4" across the seats without changing the basic chassis, wings and running-boards or facia layout. The TC was improved in detail too, the sidescreens now had flaps to facilitate hand signalling, the electrical equipment was also updated with the twin 6 volt batteries removed from the underfloor position of the TB to a bulkhead box containing a large 12 volt battery.

There were also changes to the suspension, hydraulic lever arm dampers were fitted and the road springs were mounted in shackles rather than the traditional sliding trunnions. This change allowed the use of war-proven rubber suspension bushes which gave smoother quieter feel to the car as did the fitment of rubber engine mountings. Otherwise it was exactly the same as the 1936 design of the MG TA which started the T series line. Within 5 weeks of the official end of the war in October 1945, The MG Car Company announced the TC Midget and by the end of that year had proudly produced 81 examples which was no mean feat as so many materials were in short supply, especially sheet steel. The car sold exceptionally well, a large number were exported to Commonwealth countries, particularly Australia and South Africa, which was not surprising as MGs had sold there in quantity before the war. What was surprising however was that there was immense interest in the United States and it can be stated that the MG TC was responsible for starting the American craze for the British Sportscar. Nearly 2000 cars were exported to the United States and Abingdon had deemed the potential sufficient to warrant the development of a special North American model, still in right hand drive form but with chrome bumpers and flashing indicators. The effect that the TC had on America was unbelievable as it introduced the pleasures of sports car ownership to people who had never experienced it before and it opened up the market for many more imported cars to follow.

One notable customer in England for the TC was the Duke of Edinburgh who owned one before marrying Princess Elizabeth, the future Queen, in 1947. Sales were going from strength to strength which saw over 1600 produced in 1946 rising to a peak of over 3000 during 1948. In total exactly 10,000 were produced between 1945 and 1949. Pressure was soon exerted by the Americans for an updated version of the TC and in 1950 Abingdon responded with TD in 1950. This car had an all-new chassis, with rack and pinion steering and independent front suspension, altogether a vast improvement with fairly dramatic styling changes, the first in 13 years. The 1947 TC featured belongs to Tony Newbold of Nottingham.

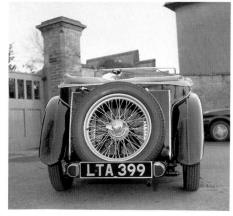

TC

SPECIFICATION

Engine
Type: 10.97 hp in line water cooled.
No. of cylinders: 4.
Bore/stroke: 66.5 x 90mm
Capacity: 1,250cc
Valve operation: Push rod operated overhead valves.
Carburation: Twin SU semi-downdraught.
Compression Ratio: 7.5 to 1.
Power output: 54.4 bhp at 5,200 rpm.
Max Torque: 64 lb/ft at 2,700 rpm.

Drive Train
Clutch: Borg and Beck single dry plate
Transmission: Four speed manual gearbox, synchromesh on 2nd, 3rd and top.

Chassis
Frame: Twin side members and cross members.
Wheelbase: 7' 10''
Track (front): 3' 9''
Track (rear): 3' 9''
Length 11' 7''
Width: 4' 8''
Suspension (front): Half elliptic springs, beam axle.
Rear: Half elliptic springs, live axle.
Brakes: Lockheed 9'' drums all round.
Tyre size: 19 x 4.50
Wheels: wire spoke.

Performance
Maximum speed: 78 mph
Acceleration: 0-60 27.25 secs
Maximum speed in each gear: 1st - 22.6, 2nd - 39.2, 3rd - 56.6, top 78.0.
Fuel Consumption: approx 27 mpg.
Number built: 10,000.
Cost new in 1947: £412 10s. 0d plus purchase tax of £114 6s. 8d, Road tax £13 0s 0d.

Y Type Saloon

When production of the MG TC resumed at Abingdon after the war, plans were also well advanced for the production of a new MG saloon which had originally been designed during the period 1937 to 1939 for introduction in 1941. The MG Y type or one and a quarter litre saloon as it was sometimes known was really an MG version of the Morris Eight series E four door saloon and was a pre-war project that Syd Enever and Cowley suspension designer Alec Issigonis had been working on in 1937. The all-steel body resembled that of the Morris but had suitable modifications to the front and rear end to give a traditional MG 'look' with specially swept tail and rear wings. A new and rather more traditional nose included a vertical chrome slat radiator. The chassis however was completely different. The frame was of welded box section and underslung at the rear with leaf spring suspension. Front suspension was independent with coil springs and wishbones which was somewhat a rarity at that time and the first such application to a Nuffield Organisation production car. Torsion bars as used on the earlier R type were not utilised and did not re-appear for many years later until the launch of the MGC in 1967. Rack and pinion steering was introduced for the first time on an MG and was mechanically more precise than the Bishop cam type used on the earlier T series models.

Solid and robust, the Y type chassis was to form the basis for many future sports models however like so many pre-war designs the car was far too heavy for its engine with the car weighing in at 20 hundredweights some 440 lbs heavier than the TC. With only a single SU carburettor and a detuned version of the 1250cc XPAG engine, as used in the TB, that had a lower compression ratio and different valve timing, performance was far from brisk. It was however an ideal cruising car with a high degree of comfort and a touch of luxury. The gearbox was a four speed synchromesh unit with remote control that was renowned for it's positive change and the rear axle was of conventional MG design.

The whole car was extremely well appointed by post-war depression standards and was very much in the style of the pre-war S, V and W saloons and tourers. It was welcomed by both the motoring press and public alike when it was announced in the spring of 1947 priced at £671 11s 8d. The car subsequently enjoyed sales success both at home and abroad and although of compact dimensions and not particularly roomy, the ride and roadholding standards were excellent and at the time was judged exceptionally comfortable compared to many of its contemporaries. There were many features fitted as standard on the Y type such as the Smiths 'Jackall' four wheel hydraulic jacking system. This consisted of four hydraulic jacks located adjacent to the wheels that could be lowered all at the same time to support the car entirely free of the ground, this enabled wheel changes and general maintenance. The front could also be raised independently and vice versa. The hydraulic pump was located on the nearside of the engine bulkhead and was activated by a hand operated lever. Other features worthy of note were the opening front screen and sliding steel sunroof together with an adjustable telescopic steering column and rear window blind.

The Y Saloon was never designated YA but over the years has adopted the title from owners and enthusiasts. It sold quite well though it

could not hope to equal the runaway export success of the TC and TD Midget models. 6,158 examples were produced at Abingdon through until 1951 when a slightly improved version the YB was introduced. This car had slightly smaller wheels (15" instead of 16") and a front anti-roll bar was fitted. Larger heavy duty shock absorbers were employed together with a hypoid rear axle and uprated brakes, all of which greatly improved the car's performance on the road with better handling and

stopping power. Like its predecessor, the YB had to counter very little by way of competition from other manufacturers and despite the uninspiring appearance the Y series MG achieved a production figure of well over 8000 units by the end of production in 1953.

Worthy of mention is the production of an open touring version of the Y type which was launched at the Motor Show in the autumn of 1948. The YT as it was known was an open topped full four seater. This car was lighter and

slightly quicker than the saloon versions powered by a TC specification engine of 1250 cc. The car unfortunately was not greeted with enthusiasm due to its rather bulky appearance and was reminiscent of an Army General's staff car. Most of the production (877) were exported with Australia as the main market. The YT utilised the same chassis as the YA with the 54bhp twin carburettor TC engine as power unit. The dashboard was different being somewhat similar to that of the TC. It was assumed that most of the YTs were built in left hand drive specification for the export markets but in fact most were right hand drive versions destined for Australia rather than the USA . Low volume production of the YT continued through until 1950 and was one of the last open tourers of its kind to be made apart from that produced by the Singer Motor Company.

Y TYPE SALOON

PRB 346

SPECIFICATION

Engine: XPAG 4 cylinder in line, water cooled.
Bore & Stroke: 66.5mm x 90mm
Capacity: 1250cc
Valve gear: Pushrod overhead.
Compression ratio: 7:2:1
Power Output: 46bhp @ 4,800rpm
Carburation: Single SU 1¼″ semi downdraught.

Clutch: 7¼″ Borg & Beck single dry plate.
Gearbox: 4 speed, synchro on 2nd, 3rd and top.
Suspension: Front: Independent coil and wishbone. Rear: Half elliptic.
Shock absorbers: Luvax-Girling piston type.
Brakes: Lockheed hydraulic with 9″ drums.
Wheelbase: 8′3″
Track: front 3′11⅜″ rear: 4′2″
Steering: Direct acting rack and pinion.
Wheels and tyres: Bolt-on ventilated disc. 5.25 x 16″
Weight: 20 cwt
Production: Early 1947 to late 1953.
Number produced: YA: 6158. YB: 1301. YT: 877
Performance: 0-60mph in 29.3 secs.
Fuel consumption: approx 27mpg.
Cost new in 1951: £565 plus purchase tax £315 7s 9d.

YB Saloon

It was in the spring of 1947 that the 1¼ litre MG saloons started to leave the factory gates at Abingdon, better known as the Y series cars, they were often thought of as the MG version of the Morris Eight series E four door saloon. It is true that the MG was based on the Morris 8 which provided the basic body shell pressings, however the power unit was sourced from the Morris 10 series M car. The prototype Y type was originally constructed in 1939 and at this stage the MG was expected to be known as the MG Ten to be launched at the 1940 Motor Show. The car was conceived as an smaller addition to the existing range of MG saloons which were the S, V and W models. It was intended to compete with other similar products on offer from competitors such as Singer, Riley, Triumph and Sunbeam Talbot. The 2nd World war intervened in the development and production of the Y series cars as Abingdon workers turned their skills to more pressing things like building tanks and armoured cars!. Syd Enever and Alec Issigonis had started work on the project codenamed EX 166 as early as 1937 and the development work that had gone into fitting independent suspension onto pre-war MG racing cars was adapted for use on the new Y series cars, in fact the Y saloon was one of the first British production cars to be fitted with such a suspension arrangement and it was considered very advanced for the day. Rack and pinion steering was also introduced for the first time on an MG as it was mechanically more precise that the Bishop Cam type used on the earlier T types.

The all-new chassis was of solid and robust construction and was to form the basis for many future sports MGs to come. It consisted of longitudinal box sections between the axles joined by four cross members with the engine and gearbox mounted forward in the chassis to give good weight distribution and allow room for rear seating within the wheelbase. There was a weight penalty however for such a solid chassis with the finished car weighing in at over a ton, this precluded any meaningful performance. With only a single SU carburettor and a detuned version of the 1250 cc XPAG engine as used in the TB that had a lower compression ratio and different valve timing, performance was far from brisk. It was however deemed an ideal cruising car with a high level of comfort coupled with a touch of luxury. The gearbox was a four speed unit with synchromesh on 2nd, 3rd and top, transferring power to the rear wheels via a spiral bevel banjo-type rear axle as fitted to the Morris 10. There were many features fitted as standard to the Y type such as the Smiths 'Jackall' four wheel hydraulic system. Four rams pushed downwards on the ground activated by a hand operated pump unit mounted on the bulkhead. This enabled the driver to raise the whole car off the ground enabling easy wheel changing and other maintenance. The front could be raised independently and vice versa if required. Other features worthy of

note were the sliding steel sunroof and top-hinged opening front windscreen which afforded a good variety of ventilation. A telescopically adjustable steering column, adjustable seats and a rear window blind that could be operated by the driver were welcome attributes.

The body of the Y type was very much of Morris 8 parentage with minor modifications and different swept wings both front and rear. The body had provision for a luggage compartment with exterior bootlid and had a separate compartment under the boot floor to house the spare wheel and tools. This compartment was accessed by removing a small panel under the bootlid. It was commonplace before the war and generally fashionable to have no external bootlid with all luggage being loaded through the driver or passenger door and stowed behind the seats. The fitting of a bootlid had a twofold purpose to ease the carrying of luggage and to increase the capacity or size of luggage that could be carried. With

the bootlid in the down position, bulky items could be strapped to the horizontal bootlid to be transported in relative safety! The Y type was welcomed by both the public and motoring press alike when it was announced in the spring of 1947 priced at £525 plus purchase tax of £146 11s 8d. The car sold well both at home and abroad but it could not hope to match the runaway export success of the TD and TD Midget models. 6,158 models were produced at Abingdon up to 1951 when the improved version the YB was introduced.

It was towards the end of 1951 that Abingdon planned some considerable mechanical changes to the Y type. The YB as it was officially designated was to go on sale in 1952 and it was hoped that these changes would give the car a new lease of life. Increased braking efficiency was a welcome improvement, a completely new Lockheed braking system was installed which had twin leading shoes on the front. Then a hypoid back axle as fitted to the TD Midget replaced the ageing Morris 10 unit. A heavier duty 8" diameter clutch was substituted for the old 7¼" unit. Other changes which improved handling, as the car tended to oversteer, were the fitting of heavy duty shock absorbers at the rear, a thicker anti-roll bar was fitted and the diameter of the road wheels was reduced from 16" to 15". In order to accommodate the smaller wheels the rear wing profile was changed and made deeper between the top of the wheel arch and the top of the wing. At the same time the spare wheel aperture and lid were made 1" larger. A more up to date voltage regulator was fitted together with twin windtone horns and chrome bumper overriders were made available as extras. The YB was only produced in relatively small numbers with 1,301 cars being produced before production ceased at the latter end of 1953. The YB cost £989 including purchase tax and was offered in a choice of six colours, two of which were metallic finishes. The featured YB belonging to Dave Keen is in everyday use and looks well in its original metallic Silver Streak Grey paintwork.

YB SALOON

SPECIFICATION

Engine Type: XPAG, 4 cylinder in line, water cooled.

Bore & Stroke: 66.5 mm x 90 mm

Capacity: 1250 cc

Valve Gear: Pushrod overhead

Compression Ratio: 7.2:1

Power output: 46bhp @ 4,800 rpm

Maximum Torque: 702 lb/in @ 2,400 rpm

Carburation: Single SU type H2 1¼"

Transmission: Clutch: Borg & Beck 8" dry plate

Gearbox: 4 speed, synchromesh on 2nd, 3rd and top

Suspension: Front: Independent with coil springs Rear: Half elliptic springs

Shock absorbers: Luvax Girling piston type

Brakes: Lockheed hydraulic with 9" drums

Wheels & tyres: Bolt-on ventilated disc 5.50 x 15"

Steering: Direct acting rack and pinion

Wheelbase: 8' 3"

Track: Front; 3' 11⅜" Rear; 4' 2"

Weight: 20 cwts 3 qtrs

Production: 1952-53

Number produced: 1,301

Performance: 0-60 mph; 30.4 secs

Fuel consumption: 26.5 mpg

Maximum speed: 71.4 mph

Cost new in 1952: £989 5s 6d

YT Tourer

Up until 1935 the MG Car Company and Morris Motors were essentially separate companies although both were owned by Sir William Morris. Following a takeover in 1935 the two concerns were incorporated under the umbrella of the Nuffield organisation which also owned other marques such as Wolseley and Riley. From then on the derivation of MG

models was to be from several camps in order to rationalise and to introduce a common parts policy. Two years later the MG model range included two saloons, the SA and VA and a year later the larger WA saloon appeared which sported a 2,561 cc engine. These saloons were introduced to compete with the large saloons available from S.S. Cars (who later became known as Jaguar Cars Ltd). In the Morris camp, there was a Ten Series M saloon available during 1938 to be followed by the launch of the Eight Series E at the October Motor Show. MG needed a compact size saloon to compete with the cars offered by Singer, Riley, Triumph and Sunbeam-Talbot and to compliment their S, V, and W range. The MG Y Type Saloon or one and a quarter litre MG Saloon as it was better known was on the drawing board between 1937 and 1939 ready for introduction in 1941. Codenamed EX 166, it was really an MG version of the Morris Eight Series E and was designed by Syd Enever and Alec Issigonis in the Morris design studio at Cowley. The war put paid to plans for a 1941 launch and the car did not see serious production until 1947.

The all steel body closely resembled the Morris, but had suitable modifications to the front and rear to give the traditional appearance of its MG forerunners. With its specially swept tail and rear wings together with the distinctive vertical chrome slatted front radiator grille, this was definitely from the MG camp. Alec Issigonis was a suspension design specialist and he was able to introduce for the first time on a British production car, an independent front suspension system which consisted of a coil spring and wishbone. Another first was the employment of rack and pinion steering instead of the Bishop cam type and the Y type was the first Nuffield car to be so equipped. The separate chassis was completely new and differed from the Morris equivalent with the frame being of welded box section with four cross members and it was underslung at the rear with leaf spring suspension. Damping was effected by means of Luvax Girling double lever arm, piston type dampers at the front with single arm dampers at the rear. A very worthwhile addition to the chassis design was the fitting of a Jackall hydraulic jacking system. This system had been incor-

porated on the larger pre-war MG saloons and was fitted as standard on the Y type.

Solid and robust the Y Type chassis was to form the basis for many future MG sports models, however like so many pre-war designs the car was too heavy for its engine. Powered by the XPAG engine of 1250 cc as used in the TB Midget, the unit only had a single carburettor and thus the power output was a meagre 46 bhp @ 4,800 rpm. With the car weighing in at nearly 21 cwts, it was some 440 lbs heavier than the TC, therefore performance was far from brisk. It was however an ideal cruising car with a high degree of comfort and luxury. Power was transferred to the rear wheels via a four speed gearbox with synchromesh on second third and top. Transmission to the banjo-type back axle

was through a Hardy Spicer tubular propshaft with needle roller universal joints. Braking was by means of a Lockheed hydraulic system acting on 9" diameter drums front and rear. The whole car was extremely well appointed by post war depression standards and was very much in the style of the pre-war S, V and W saloons and tourers.

With a luxury leather interior and walnut dash board, it received a warm welcome from the motoring press and public alike when it was announced in the spring of 1947 at a price of £671 including purchase tax. The car enjoyed very good sales both on the home market and abroad and although of compact dimensions and not particularly roomy the Y type gave a smooth ride with excellent roadholding and at the time was considered exceptionally comfortable compared to its rivals. Such features as an opening front windscreen, telescopically adjustable steering column and rear window blind all enhanced the specification of what

was already a luxury vehicle.

It is believed that the conversion of the Y type saloon to an open tourer by a Swiss coachbuilder may have influenced MG into producing their own version. The YT as it was to be known was launched at the 1948 Motor Show at an asking price of £525. For this sporty Y type, the power was increased by the addition of twin semi-downdraught SU carburettors and the fitting of the camshaft used in the TC Midget. Power was up by 8.5 bhp from 46 to 54.5. Thus top speed was increased from 70 mph on the saloon to 76 mph on the tourer. The YT was to be offered for export only and as a result the body was adapted for easy conversion to left hand drive specification. The tourer was quite different to the saloon as not just a saloon with the roof removed. The doors which were reduced to only two, were larger and deeply cut away to give the sporty look, whilst the interior was still able to accommodate four seats easily. There were changes to the dashboard and fascia which resembled that of the TC with a large rev counter in front of the driver and the passenger facing a similar sized speedometer. The use of leather for trim and seating was standard with the front seats tilting to allow access to the rear seats. The windscreen folded flat in true MG tradition, whilst the hood folded neatly away behind the rear seats with a close fitting cover.

The YT was one of the last four seat open tourers to be produced by MG and was in production between 1948 and mid 1950 with only 877 examples leaving the Abingdon factory. Of those, it is recorded that 874 were intended directly for export, however 42 cars remained in Britain. The featured car is in the ownership of David Bryant.

YT TOURER

SPECIFICATION

Engine

Type: XPAG 4 cylinder in line, water cooled

Bore & Stroke: 66.5mm x 90 mm

Capacity: 1250 cc

Valve gear: Pushrod overhead

Compression ratio: 7.2:1

Power output: 54.5 bhp @ 5,200 rpm

Maximum torque:765 lb/ in @ 2,600 rpm

Carburation: Twin SU type H2 1.25" dia

Transmission

Clutch: 7.25" dia

Borg & Beck single dry plate

Gearbox: 4 speed, synchromesh on 2nd, 3rd and top gear

Suspension

Front; independent with coil springs

Rear; half elliptic leaf springs

Brakes: Lockheed hydraulic, 9" dia drums

Steering: Rack and pinion

Wheels and tyres: Bolt on ventilated disc 5.25 x 16"

Weight: 18cwt 3qrs

Performance

Max speed: 76 mph

TD Midget

The MG TD can rightfully be described as the most popular of all the T series Midgets, following closely in the tracks of the TC Midget which was the car that put MG on a firm footing in the United States. The fact that the TC had become an overnight success in the American market helped secure a bright future for MG both at home and abroad. But whilst the Americans were still buying the TC in substantial numbers there were calls for a bigger and better updated car. It is worth noting that during 1948 and 1949 which was when the TC was at its peak of popularity, many changes were taking place in the Nuffield group with major management alterations and the new board transferring the production of Rileys from Coventry to Abingdon in the interests of rationalisation. By the summer of 1949 the production of the TC was outnumbered by the manufacture of non-sports car models such as the Riley one and a quarter litre and the two and a half litre with the production lines running parallel to those of the Y type saloons and unsuccessful YT tourer.

Because of the cool reception for the YT tourer it became clear in 1949 that overseas customers for MG sports cars particularly the Americans wanted something a bit more modern and sophisticated than the TC. Jack Tatlow who was new to the MG management and an ex-Riley man was set to work with Abingdon staff to come up with proposals for a new model to replace the TC. Abingdon was devoid of any investment due to all available money going to Cowley to develop new models there. However Syd Enever, Alec Hounslow and Cecil Cousins commenced work with a small design team to produce a prototype. This was all achieved in the space of two weeks without committing a pencil to the drawing board. Basically 5" was removed from the centre section of a YA saloon chassis frame and the two halves were welded together. A TC body was chopped up and stitched together and placed on the chassis and the end result was a rough and ready prototype that was acceptable to the Nuffield Organisation. The drawing office at Cowley then prepared accurate drawings from the prototype ready to put the car into production.

The design team would no doubt liked to have produced something more sophisticated but bearing in mind the financial constraints on development the end result was a car that made commercial technical and product planning sense. Syd Enever decided that the new car should employ a more rigid chassis frame that would not distort under extreme bending and torsional stress and that it should have independent front suspension providing a more comfortable ride. Together with the Y type's advanced rack and pinion steering the car was far easier to handle and the overall package was a car salesman's dream. Another benefit incorporated into the design was the fact that the car could readily be assembled as a left hand drive version for the lucrative export markets.

Underneath the body the Y type origins were fairly obvious with the large boxed frame chassis rails forming a very rigid platform for the independent suspension which was an exact copy of the Y type set up but utilising larger dampers. At the rear the chassis departed from its saloon car ancestor in that the frame swept up and over the rear axle instead of being underslung. The rear axle was of modern hypoid design borrowed from Morris and

Wolseley contemporaries and the gearbox was a Y type unit with a remote control gear stick. The XPAG/TD engine although bearing a

strong resemblance to the TC engine was in fact also derived from the Y type XPAG/SC engine. It is true to say that the XPAG engines were all essentially the same but on the TD version the clutch housing, dynamo, sump, rocker cover, starter motor and engine mounts were all straight from the Y type.

The TD body was no doubt inspired by earlier MG two seaters but it was considerably wider than earlier models to give more elbow room. The car was welcomed as it was the first MG since 1936 to incorporate some major styling changes. Every panel was different to that of the TC and the fascia although new, remained strictly traditional as did the separate flowing front wings, running boards, separate headlamps and the characteristic vertical slat MG radiator. A centrally hinged bonnet and exposed slab fuel tank with spare wheel carrier at the rear completed the package. Other features that were still thought to be important and in keeping with MG tradition were the cutaway doors, folding screen with wiper motor bolted to the passenger side top rail and basic slot-in side screen weather protection. The classic coach built type body panels were mounted on to the traditional ash wooden frame. In the cockpit facilities remained fairly basic with no provision for a fresh air heater or a radio and the lack of any individual adjustment on the front seats. Direction Indicators, now common on a lot of cars were noticeably absent as a standard fitment. One new addition to the TD was the fitting of sturdy chromium plated bumpers and overriders front and rear. These weighty additions were not welcomed by enthusiasts but were essentially fitted to protect the car against the poor parking techniques employed by the drivers of lumbering North American vehicles! Another controversial move was the fitting of smaller pressed steel disc wheels in place of the traditional wire spoked wheels used on the TC. This was done

because special wheels would have had to be made to accommodate the arms and links of the new rack and pinion steering and Nuffield would not have sanctioned this for use on one model alone. A strong point was made in favour of the disc wheels in so much as they were far easier to keep clean and maintain and did not distort and buckle when negotiating the potholed British roads, unlike wire wheels which were very prone to damage.

The TD was certainly less lively than its predecessor mainly due to an increase in weight of nearly 200 lbs and the fact that the engine produced the same peak power and torque as the TC ie 54bhp @ 5,200rpm. 64lb/ft @ 2,600rpm. Even with lower gearing, the lowest in fact of any T series production car independent road test figures of the day indicated that the TD was slower than the TC. Despite these minor disadvantages, would-be customers flocked to buy the car when it was introduced in late 1949. Over the 4 years the car was in production, 29,664 models were to emerge from Abingdon which was over three times the number of TCs made, it was also a new production record for MG with a staggering 10,838 being produced in 1952 alone. With raw material supply becoming easier and cheaper after the war and the huge following for British sports cars in North America, this new MG with improved roadholding and passenger comfort had immediate appeal. The main factor that helped the export sales to America was the fact that Sterling was devalued in September 1949 making British products far more attractive and cheaper to customers abroad. Despite the success story the TD was a controversial car in its day giving rise to much debate in motoring journals and at enthusiasts pub gatherings, nonetheless it has earned its place in history as a highly desirable classic British Sports Car.

TD

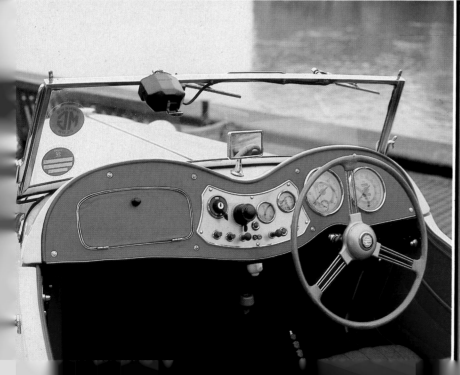

SPECIFICATION MG TD

Engine
Capacity: 1250cc
Number of cylinders: 4
Bore & stroke: 66.5mm x 90mm
Valve gear: Overhead push rod
Compression ratio: 7.25:1
BHP: 54.4 @ 5,200rpm
Torque: 64.5lb/ft @ 2,600rpm
MPH: 14.5 per 1000rpm in top gear.
Carburation: Twin semi downdraught 1½" SUs
Clutch & Gearbox: Single plate dry clutch. Four speed gearbox with synchromesh on top three gears.
Suspension: Independent front by coil and wishbone.
Non-independent rear by semi elliptic leaf springs with Luvax Girling dampers.
Brakes: Lockheed hydraulic with 2 leading shoes at front. 9" drums front and rear.
Wheels and Tyres: Bolt on disc (unperforated on early cars) Tyres 5.50 x 15"
Track: 3'11⅜" front. 4'2" rear.
Number built: 1949-1953: 29,664
Performance: 0-60mph: 18.2 secs
Top speed: 78.3mph
Fuel consumption: approx 26.7 miles per gallon.
Prices new in 1953: £500 plus £221 19s 2d purchase tax. Total £751 19s 2d.

TD Midget MK2

The TD is often described as the most popular of the T series Midgets and it followed very closely in the tracks of the TC. It was the TC that gave MG a strong foothold in the United States and helped secure a bright future for MG both at home and abroad. The car was virtually an overnight success and sold very well indeed but it was not long before there were calls for a bigger and better, more modern replacement. The TC was selling in substantial numbers during 1948/49 and was at the height of its popularity. At this time there was a transformation going on within the Nuffield with many management changes and alterations to production policy. The new board moved the manufacture of Rileys from Coventry to Abingdon in the interests of rationalisation and by mid-1949 the production of Rileys outstripped that of the current MG models. Alongside the Rileys, TC's, Y saloons and YT Tourers were being made, but it soon became evident that a replacement model was needed, even though the TC was selling well. The open top version of the Y saloon, the YT tourer (which was aimed principally at the export market) had received a very cool reception and there were now calls particularly from the Americans for a more modern and sophisticated replacement for the TC and YT.

Abingdon was devoid of investment at this time, with all available money being pumped into Cowley to develop new models for Austin, Morris and Wolseley. Syd Enever and his design team, set about the task of designing a new car and with minimal budget, managed in true Abingdon style, to produce a prototype in the space of two weeks for presentation to the Nuffield board. All this was done without committing a pencil to the drawing board and quite simply was achieved by removing 5" from the centre section of a YA saloon chassis and re-welding the two halves together. A TC body was chopped up and restyled, affixed to the chassis and the end result was a rough and ready prototype that gained the Nuffield board approval. This exercise proved that a brand new model could be produced very quickly, utilising many existing components and that a costly and lengthy development programme could be avoided. The Cowley drawing office prepared accurate drawings ready to put the car into production before the year end and thus the TD Midget was born. Many regard the TD as being a direct descendent of its forerunner the TC. This is certainly true visually as there are many styling similarities, but underneath the skin the two cars are completely different.

The TD's Y type origins were immediately apparent with the large boxed frame chassis rails forming a very rigid platform for the independent suspension that was an exact copy of the Y type set up, but utilising larger dampers. At the rear the chassis departed from its saloon car ancestor in as much as the frame swept up and over the rear axle, instead of being underslung. The rear axle was of modern hypoid design, borrowed from Morris and Wolseley contempories and the gearbox was a Y type unit with a remote control gearstick. The XPAG/TD engine, although bearing a strong resemblance to the TC was in fact also derived from the Y type XPAG/SC engine. It is true to say that all XPAG engines are essentially the same, however on the TD version, the clutch housing, dynamo, sump, rocker cover, starter motor and engine mounts were all taken straight from the Y type. The TD body was in keeping with its sports car ancestors but was considerably wider than earlier models to give more elbow room in the cockpit. The car was welcomed, if only that it was the first MG since 1936 to adopt major styling changes. Every panel was different to that of the TC and with a car that was considerably bigger all round there was obviously a weight penalty. The TD weighed in at some 200 lbs heavier than its predecessor and with the same power output from the engine and an identical rear axle ratio to the TC there was in fact a slight downgrading of performance, which did not bode well amongst the enthusiasts. Even with lower gearing, the lowest in fact of any T series car, independent road tests indicated that the TD was slower than the TC. Despite this many people flocked to buy the car when it was introduced in late 1949. Over the 4 years that the car was in production, 29,664 models were to emerge from Abingdon, which was over three times the production run of the TC.

Shortly after the TD went into production the factory responded to demands for more power and better handling and introduced a modified version known as the TD Mark II. To the untrained eye there appeared little difference between the two models, however because the Mark II was produced in relatively low numbers (just under 3.5% of total production) and was a definite improvement over the standard TD, it has become very much a collectors car. There has been confusion over the years amongst TD owners, some of whom believed that they owned a TD Mark II when in fact they did not. Many have been disappointed to learn that the configuration XPAG TD 2 on their engine did not mean that their car was a TD Mark II . The only difference between XPAG TD 2 and XPAG/TD is the fact that the former has larger clutch, flywheel and housing. The simplest way to determine whether a TD is a Mark II or not, is in the car number, all standard TD's (there is no such thing as a TD Mark I) commence their number with the prefix TD and all Mark II's commence TD/c.

The main differences lay in the engine which gained an extra 5.5% in power and in the suspension which was supplemented with Andrex friction dampers at each wheel. The normal Luvax Girling dampers were retained and the combined effect was to give the car far better cornering and a slightly stiffer ride. On the engine side the compression ratio was raised from 7.25:1 to 8.1 :1 and the head was fitted with larger valves. Larger Twin SU H4 1 1/2" carburettors were fitted on a modified inlet manifold. Dual SU fuel pumps were installed to ensure continuity of petrol supply at sustained high speeds. Initially this is all that was done but some later cars had a different distributor with changed advance curve that better suited the higher compression ratio and latterly the engine adopted a larger air cleaner. Externally there was nothing to distinguish the TD Mark II

from the standard TD until towards the end of production when it was decided that the TD Mark II should be set apart from the rest. This was achieved with a slight bulge in the bonnet side panel to accommodate the larger air intake pipe, Mark II badges on each of the bonnet side panels with another mounted centrally on the rear bumper and the vertical slats in the radiator grille were to become chromium plated. There was also a change in the background colour of the MG motifs from brown and cream to black and white and the addition of a passenger grab handle on the dashboard. Mistakenly enthusiasts talk of bucket seats as being an identifying feature of the Mark II, however this is simply because Abingdon prepared a press car with such seats, no production cars were ever fitted with these although they could be obtained as optional extras. All of the components making up the TD Mark II specification could be purchased and fitted to the standard TD which resulted in a few "replica" TD Mark II's.

27

TD MKII

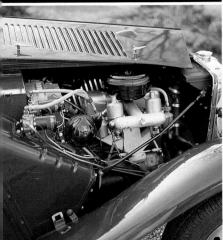

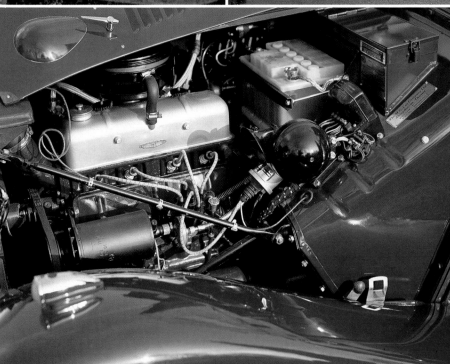

SPECIFICATION

Engine: 4 cylinder in line
Capacity: 1250cc
Bore & Stroke: 66.5mm x 90mm
Valve gear: Overhead pushrod
Compression ratio: 8.0:1
Power output: 60 bhp @ 5,500 rpm
Carburation: Twin 1.5" SU H4 semi downdraught
Clutch: Single dry plate.
Gearbox: Four forward speed with synchromesh on top three
Suspension: Front; independent coil and wishbone
Rear; Half elliptic leaf springs, live rear axle. To supplement the hydraulic lever arm shock absorbers, an additional set of Andrex friction dampers were also fitted.
Brakes: Lockheed hydraulic 9" drum front & rear
Wheels: Bolt on perforated steel disc.
Performance: 0-60 mph; 16.5 secs.
Top speed: 83 mph
Number built: 1,022.

TF Midget 1250

The MG TF was launched at the 1953 Motor show at Earls Court in London alongside the all new ZA Magnette Saloon. The MG TF was greeted with mixed reactions by enthusiasts and journalists alike, for it was heavily criti-

cised at the time for being old fashioned, in fact one motoring writer referred to the car as "a TD with the front pushed in". Today the TF is certainly a desirable car and is hailed as the most attractive of the 'traditional MGs' commanding far higher sale values than any of its T series predecessors. The TF was introduced at a time when competitors such as Triumph produced the TR2 and Austin Healey, the 100 series. Many motoring journalists thought that the TF would be a non starter in the light of this competition, however the sales of the two TF versions, 1250 cc and 1500 cc totalled 9600 in 19 months, which considering it was only a stopgap model before the introduction of the MGA, was no mean feat.

The TF was based on the same chassis and mechanical components of the TD Mark II. The centre section of the car body shell remained virtually the same as that of the TD. The most significant change was to adopt a sloping radiator grille which for the first time concealed a separate radiator. Other changes included the lowering of the centre of the scuttle and reducing the radiator grille height by over three and a half inches so that the bonnet had a marked forward slope. The front wings were also restyled to accommodate faired-in headlamps instead of the traditional bolt on fixings on the wing stays as in the TD. The rear of the car received some general restyling with modifications to the fuel tank and spare wheel mounting to help tidy up the overall appearance of the car.

In keeping with the external modifications the cockpit layout was quite radically changed to that of its predecessor. Individual adjustable seats were provided in place of the normal bench type seating. The facia panel was completely new with a welcome return to octagonal instrumentation. This was positioned centrally to allow easy construction of either a left or a

right hand drive vehicle, many customers however complained that the rev counter was too far away for easy reading. Two useful gloveboxes were provided on either side of the instrument panel which also housed the parking knobs for the windscreen wipers. In many ways the TF had advanced over its forerunners with innovative additions but despite the fairly comprehensive instrumentation with oil pressure gauge, temperature gauge, ammeter, clock etc, there was still no fuel gauge which surprised many would be purchasers. Another retrograde step was to make the bonnet sides fixed and only the top of the bonnet could be hinged up to work on the engine, this made normally easy jobs quite difficult and tedious.

The car was supplied with steel disc wheels as standard, although centre lock wire spoke wheels were available as an optional extra, other extras included a badge bar, fog lamps and a chrome luggage carrier.

On introduction you could purchase a TF for the basic price of £550 plus purchase tax of £30 5s. 10d. Its nearest rival the Triumph TR2 could be bought for a basic price of £555 which at only £5 more, proved in some potential customers eyes, more of a bargain especially as the TR2 was capable of more than 100 mph compared to the 'flat out' speed of the TF at little more than 80 mph. Mechanically the TF proved most reliable and also felt very good to drive with impeccable roadholding and handling, however the car was embarrassingly slow compared to its competitors both in acceleration and top speed.

Something needed to be done to overcome the lack of appeal caused by poor performance. There was no possibility of a body restyle to overcome bad aerodynamics as EX 182 (to be known as the MGA) was already well advanced for launch in 1955. The only practical way to improve the car without too much investment would be to provide more power, as the car could not easily be made lighter. Utilising aluminium panels, would involve huge expense making it uncompetitive with its rival. It was decided as a stop gap measure to fit a larger more powerful engine which was a modified version of the XPAG unit bored out to 1,466cc and designated as engine type XPEG. Externally there were no visual clues other than engine numbers to distinguish the two power units and there were no other identifying features on the car other than two '1500' motifs on the bonnet sides. The larger power unit did give the TF a small boost in sales mainly in the United states and out of the 3,400 produced only a handful were sold in the UK. Sadly the TF was the last of the T series Midget line before the introduction of the MGA. Many workers at the Abingdon factory knew that MG would rather have not produced the TF if the MGA launch could have been brought forward to 1953, but I am sure that many enthusiasts would agree that the world would have been deprived of a most desirable classic MG.

TF

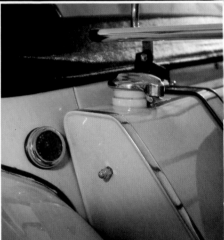

OXJ 506

SPECIFICATION MG TF 1250

Produced: October 1953 to November 1954
Numbers Built: 6,200
Engine: BMC/NUFFIELD XPAG Type Water Cooled
No. of Cylinders: 4
Bore/Stroke: 66.5 x 90mm
CC: 1250cc
Compression Ratio:8.0:1
BHP: 57 bhp @ 5,500 rpm
Maximum torque: 65 lbft @ 3000 rpm
Carburation: Twin semi downdraught constant vacuum SU H4 carburrettors.
Drive Train: Clutch: Dry Plate
Transmission: Four Speed manual with synchromesh on 2nd, 3rd and top gear.
Chassis: Separate box section chassis frame.
Wheelbase: 7' 10''
Track (front): 3' 11.4''
(rear) : 4' 2''
Suspension: Independent wishbone and coil on front.
Half elliptic springs with live axle on rear.
Steering: Rack and Pinion.
Brakes: Lockheed hydraulic front and rear drums with no vacuum servo assistance.
Wheels and tyres: Standard pressed steel bolt on disc wheels 15'' diameter with 5.50-15 tyres Optional centre lock wire spoke wheels of same diameter and width.

PERFORMANCE

Maximum Speed: 80mph
Acceleration: 0-60 in 19 secs
Standing quarter mile: 21.5 secs
Maximum speed in each gear: 1st: 26mph, 2nd: 43mph, 3rd: 64mph.
Fuel Consumption: 25 mpg average

TF Midget 1500

Often referred to as 'the last of the square riggers' the TF gained this title due to its very strong resemblance to the pre-war Midgets. Originally launched at the 1953 Motor Show the TF was greeted with mixed reactions from enthusiasts and journalists alike. It was no secret that the TF was a stop gap measure due to a delay in putting the long awaited MGA into production. This was due entirely to Leonard Lord, the BMC Managing Director who favoured the proposal put forward by Donald Healey for his Healey 100. Healey had pipped the Abingdon men by several days which resulted in the long awaited MGA project being put on hold for at least a couple of years. Lord considered that the MGA and Healey were so similar and it was for this reason that the TF became part of MG history. Many considered that the TF was simply a revamped TD, one scathing journalist even reported that it looked like"a TD with the front pushed in". To the Abingdon engineers, led by Cecil Cousins, it was a model that was sufficiently different from its predecessors and yet continued the traditional T series classic lines. The TF was introduced at a time when other manufacturers were producing very sleek and streamlined models. The aforementioned Healey although from the same camp was seen as a direct competitor and Triumph with their TR2 were viewed in the same light. Other makes that MG had to compete with at that time were Morgan, Porsche, AC and Jaguar with their stunning XK 120. Many motoring journalists thought that the TF would be a non-starter, particularly with such a varied sports car selection available to prospective purchasers. However, even in the light of this stiff competition and the fact that the TF was only intended as a stop gap measure, sales of the two TF versions, 1250 cc and 1500 cc totalled 9,600 in 19 months which was a creditable achievement. The prototype TF was produced in true Abingdon style being put together in just a few weeks by Cecil Cousins and his team. Based on a TD chassis the prototype was built up without any reference to plans and was swiftly approved by BMC before proper working drawings were undertaken in May 1953. By September of that year the TF was put into full production.

Essentially the TF was based on the same chassis and mechanical components as the TD Mark II. The centre section of the body shell remained virtually the same as that of the TD. The most significant change was to adopt a sloping radiator grille that for the first time concealed a separate radiator. The bonnet also had a marked forward slope achieved by lowering the radiator shell by three and a half inches in relation to the scuttle top. The front wings were also restyled to accommodate faired in headlamps instead of the traditional bolt on fixings on the wing stays as on the TD. The wings in turn were faired into the bonnet sides which all in all helped to create a new streamlined image. The rear of the car received some general restyling with modifications to the fuel tank and spare wheel mounting to help tidy up the overall appearance of the car. The end result was a car very pleasing to the eye but still a little dated compared to the offerings of other manufacturers of the era. Interior wise and in keeping with the external modifications the cockpit layout was quite radically changed to that of its predecessor. A combination of items taken from the Y series saloons, the TD and some items exclusive to

the TF formed a comfortable and pleasant cockpit. Individual adjustable seats were provided in place of the normal bench type seating. The facia panel was completely new with a welcome return to octagonal instrumentation. This was positioned centrally to allow easy construction of either a left or right hand drive model, many customers complained however that the rev counter was too far away for easy reading. Despite being advanced over its predecessors with many innovative additions, there was still no fuel gauge which surprised many would be purchasers. Otherwise the instrumentation was quite comprehensive with an oil pressure gauge, temperature gauge, ammeter and clock. One other source of irritation was the fact that the bonnet sides were fixed and only the top of the bonnet could be hinged up to work on the engine. This made some normally easy jobs quite difficult and tedious.

Initially the car was launched with the faithful 1250 cc XPAG engine that made its debut in the TB Midget back in 1939. Many enthusiasts were disappointed with this as they had hoped for more power, particularly as the Triumph TR2 was capable of over 100 mph compared to the 'flat out' 80 mph achievable with the TF. Mechanically the car proved most reliable and also felt very good to drive with impeccable roadholding and handling, however the car was embarrassingly slow compared to its competitors both in acceleration and top speed. It was evident that something had to be done to overcome the lack of appeal caused by poor performance. There was no possibility of improving the aerodynamics as this would have been costly and EX 182 (codename for the MGA project) was already well advanced for launch in 1955. The only practical solution was to give the car more power, and although

thought was given to lightening the chassis and utilising aluminium panels to improve the power to weight ratio, this was rejected on cost grounds.

Late in the summer of 1954, a new 1466 cc engine was introduced to the TF designated XPEG. It was in the main very similar to its predecessor the XPAG TF. Siamesing of the cylinders allowed a larger bore in the same block and with larger pistons, stronger conrods and an increase in the compression ratio to 8.3:1, the new engine produced a meaningful 63 bhp which equated to a 10.5% increase in power. Externally there were no visual clues other

than engine numbers to distinguish the two power units and there was little on the car to give away its identity as a TF 1500, other than two discreet 'TF 1500' motifs on each of the bonnet side panels and the addition of two rear reflectors. The larger power unit did give the TF a boost in sales mainly in the United States and out of the 3,400 TF 1500's produced, only a handful were sold in the UK. It is well known that Abingdon would rather not have produced the TF, had the MGA project been given earlier approval, nonetheless the TF, and particularly the 1500 version have become one of the most desirable classic MGs.

The fine TF 1500 featured bears chassis number 0251, it is a most interesting car in as much as it is, metaphorically speaking, "the first and the last TF". It is one of two cars built up in the development workshop, with the other car carrying chassis number 0250. Most of the earlier MG models commenced their chassis number sequence with 251 which was intentionally coincident with the factory telephone number, Abingdon 251. This tradition was interrupted when chassis number 501 was assigned to the first production run TF. The feature car was built up originally in August 1953 as a 1250 cc car, retained as a development car and used very little by the factory. In fact the car was stored in a corner of the works and virtually ignored until near the end of production of the TF 1500 in April 1955. A decision was then taken to make the car into a saleable vehicle and was fitted with a 1500 engine.

TF 1500

SPECIFICATION
Engine type: XPEG.
No of cylinders: 4 in line.
Capacity: 1466 cc.
Bore & Stroke: 72mm x 90mm.
Compression ratio: 8.3:1.
Max power: 63 bhp at 5,000 rpm.
Max torque: 76 lbft at 3,000 rpm.
Carburation: Twin semi-downdraught constant vacuum SU HS4's.
Clutch: Single dry plate.
Gearbox: Four speed manual with synchromesh on 2,3 and 4.
Chassis: Steel box section overslung at rear.
Wheelbase: 7' 10".
Track: front; 3' 11.4" rear; 4' 2".
Suspension: front; independent wishbone and coil. rear; half elliptic springs with live axle.
Performance: 0-60 mph 16.3 secs.
Max speed: 88 mph.
Number built: 3,400.

ZA Magnette

Launched in 1953 at the London Motor show alongside the TF Midget, the MG ZA Magnette was greeted with mixed feelings both by enthusiasts and the motoring press alike. BMC, newly formed in 1952 after the merger with Nuffield and Austin Motors, had also mis-judged the TF, as this model too was originally greeted with disdain. Leonard Lord who became chairman and managing director of the new corporation, initially favoured the killing off of the famous Nuffield marques, namely Morris, Wolseley, Riley and MG in favour of Austin. But this he was unable to do as compensation costs to existing franchise holders would have been very costly and would have caused tremendous emotional upset in the trade and amongst the car buying public. As a result, Lord came up with an inge-nious idea which became known as "badge engineering". This meant that in future, BMC would produce basic models which could be adapted with different marque badges and trim levels at modest extra cost. This was a very clever move as it created the impression that the cars were quite different from each other. It worked well with Austin, Morris and other rele-vant marques but not so well with MG, simply because in the past most models had been unique to MG. In view of the exceptional sales achievements of MG in past years, Lord could not risk overlooking the potential and decided to try the same exercise with MG. This was achieved by allowing the cars to retain more of their own identity whilst closely associating them to at least one other car in the BMC range.

The replacement for the Y series cars was well advanced before the Nuffield/Austin merger and was in the hands of designer Gerald Palmer. Gerald was originally working for the Nuffield Organisation before the war and had in fact designed the Y type saloon that did not see production until 1947. He had a temporary move to the Jowett camp where he was responsible for the Javelin project before returning to Nuffield in 1949 to be given the brief to develop a new range of saloons for Riley, Wolseley and MG. The merger in 1952 had little effect on Palmer's work and his pro-jects were allowed to continue whilst colleague Alec Issigonis was assigned to the Morris products. Palmer designed two cars,one was a medium sized saloon that would carry the Wolseley and MG badge and the other was a far larger saloon that would sport Riley and Wolseley badges designated Pathfinder and 6/90 respectively. The smaller saloon was to be of unitary or what is better known as mono-coque construction and the MG version, which became the ZA Magnette was the first MG to employ this method of construction. Gone was the separate chassis to be replaced by a com-plete bodyshell which carried mountings for the engine gearbox and suspension. This type of construction was rapidly becoming popular in the 1950's in view of the fact that the car could be made much lighter whilst still retain-ing strength and rigidity, also unit costs were dramatically reduced when put into high vol-ume production.

The Wolseley 4/44 preceded the MG ZA Magnette by a year and was launched in 1952. The delay on the MG was to allow the new BMC 'B' Series engine to be fitted along with other newly developed components, whilst the 4/44 had the XPAG series engine handed down from the Y type. Palmer wanted to differ-entiate between the two cars and did this by

making the Wolseley the luxury car and the MG the sporting saloon. This was achieved by lowering the MG body by some two inches and changing suspension and shock absorber characteristics. This gave the MG a far more sporting appearance as well as greatly improved roadhandling. Although basically similar in appearance, in the end many of the bodypanels were different. The only ones com-mon to both cars were the roof, front doors and bootlid. The floor pan, rear doors, rear wings, front wings and sills were all different as was the bonnet arrangement. Each car had its tra-ditional front grille and on the Wolseley this was fixed in the normal fashion with the rear hinged bonnet opening in conventional man-ner, whilst the Magnette carried the grille affixed to the front bonnet edge.

The Magnette was the first MG to be fitted with the all new 'B' series engine. This twin carbu-rettor 1489 cc unit was based on the 1200 cc Austin A40 engine which was first used in 1947, however the new engine was substan-tially modified and produced a healthy 60 bhp @ 4,600 rpm. This 'B' series engine certainly made the Magnette a good performer and was far quicker than its stablemate, the Wolseley 4/44 powered by the XPAG engine that could only muster 46 bhp @ 4,800 rpm. The Wolseley was also hindered by a non-positive column gear change whilst the Magnette had a new centre floor gear lever in keeping with its sports saloon image. The rear axle was also new and had a torque reaction arm to aid axle location as rubber bushes were used exten-sively in the suspension mountings to reduce noise, improve the ride quality and reduce maintenance. Suspension was independent at the front with wishbones and coil springs and semi-elliptic springs at the rear. Large 10 inch

brakes all round catered for the increased per-formance. This very comfortable 4 seater was a civilised luxury sports saloon and despite its lukewarm reception at launch it soon became a sales success with customers loyal to the marque soon warming to it. With sales reach-ing around 6,000 units per year, the Magnette soon had a strong following and due to its superb handling and performance the car was achieving commendable results in internation-al rallies and production car races.

When production of the Magnette was well under way, Abingdon turned their efforts to the production of the all-new MGA which was launched in 1955. Whilst the MGA was fur-thering the MG tradition, the ZA Magnette was in need improvement although it had done much the same thing, albeit in a different mar-ket sector. At the latter end of 1956 the ZA gave way to the ZB which carried new refine-ments and a more powerful engine. Like so many MGs the Z series cars had been intro-duced to howls of disappointment, yet proved itself to be a thoroughly capable and much admired car with over 36,000 examples being produced. The concours ZA Magnette featured is an example of a car saved from a final rest-ing place in the scrap yard after it had been laid up for many years by it original aged lady owner. The owner is Phil Jones from Lymington.

ZA
MAGNETTE

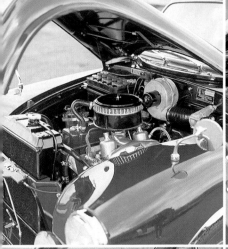
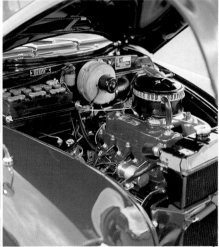

SPECIFICATION
Engine: 4 cylinder in line
Bore & Stroke: 73mm x 88.9mm
Capacity: 1489cc
Valve operation: Pushrod overhead valve
Carburation: Twin semi-downdraught SU
Power Output: 60 bhp at 4,600 rpm
Max torque: 76.1 lb/ft at 3,00 rpm
Clutch: Single dry plate
Gearbox: Part synchromesh 4 speed manual
Suspension: front; coil and wishbone rear;
half elliptic springs
Steering: Rack and pinion
Wheels: Bolt on steel disc
Brakes: Lockheed hydraulic with 10" drums
Wheelbase: 8' 6''
Track: 4' 3'' front & rear
Length: 14' 1''
Number built: ZA 12,754
ZB 23,846

ZB Varitone Magnette

In 1952 the Nuffield Organisation and the Austin Motor Company merged to form the British Motor Corporation, however this was seen more as a takeover by Austin. Lord Nuffield was retained in an honourary position as president of BMC until his death in 1963, but it was Leonard Lord, Austin's chairman and managing director who was in total charge of the corporation from the outset. It was well known that he would personally have liked to have killed off all the Nuffield marques of Morris, Wolseley, Riley and MG in favour of Austin. Because Nuffield and Austin dealers had had such close ties in the past and due to there being so many of them, it would have been very costly to compensate those dealers who would have lost their franchises, which would have been a necessary step if all BMC products only carried the Austin badge. BMC could not afford to adopt this course of action and Lord came up with an ingenious idea which became known as "Badge Engineering". This meant that in future BMC would produce basic models which could be adapted with different marque badges and trim at very little extra cost. This was a clever move, as it created the impression that the cars were quite different from each other. It worked well with Austin, Morris and other relevant marques but not so well with MG, because in the past most models had been unique to MG. In view of the exceptional sales achievements of MG in past years, Lord could not afford to overlook the potential and decided to do the same thing with MG, whilst allowing the cars to retain more of their own identity closely connected to at least one other car in the BMC range .

The first move in the rationalisation plan was to scrap Nuffield engines, utilising 'A' and 'B' series engines in many cars. At the same time work started on standardising bodyshells. The Wolseley 4/44 was launched in 1952 with the XPAG 1250 cc engine and was modified to take the 'B' series unit with MG radiator and badging to become known as the Z series Magnette. Introduced in October 1953, the name Magnette was revived having last been used in 1936. The car was introduced at the 1953 Motor Show alongside a new version of the MG TF. The ZA Magnette was really a replacement for the YB saloon which had sold well but had very rapidly become dated. However, a thinly disguised Wolseley that was being presented as an MG upset a lot of MG purists, and there were many lively exchanges in the letters columns of the leading motoring journals of the time! "A perversion of the famous name" was one such comment that was commonly heard, but many had forgotten that the first Magnette was a saloon aimed at a very similar type of customer.

The Magnette was completely different to any previous MG and was to many people a pleasing saloon of Italian design origin. It was the first MG to employ a body of monocoque construction, that is to say it was not built on a separate chassis, with the bodyshell providing mountings for the engine, gearbox and suspension. This type of construction was rapidly becoming popular in the 1950's in view of the fact that the whole car could be made much lighter but still retaining strength, also when mass produced, the unit costs dropped dramatically. One of the advantages of this type of construction was that the passenger compartment floor could be sited much lower in the vehicle, along with the engine and drive train, thus giving a lower centre of gravity, producing far better handling.

This very comfortable 4 seater had independent front suspension with wishbones and coil springs and a live rear axle located by a torque arm. This torque arm was needed because rubber bushes were used extensively in the suspension mountings to reduce noise, improve the quality of ride and reduce maintenance. Altogether the car was very civilised

and became an immediate success despite the criticism it received upon its launch. With the new 'B' series 1498 cc engine, the Magnette was far faster than the Wolseley, producing 60 bhp @ 4600 rpm. This engine was not liked initially at Abingdon, but was soon to demonstrate versatility and reliability through its enormous tuning potential. The car also easily out-performed its YB predecessor, due to the excellent roadholding characteristics and was to obtain commendable results in international rallies and production car races later on. The new Magnette sold well at around 6000 units per year, with its luxurious leather interior and 'octagonal like' instrumentation, customers loyal to the marque soon warmed to the car.

The introduction of the Magnette heralded the start of a revolution at Abingdon in which the factory changed from being a works where cars were built from hundreds of small components to one where they were simply assembled, in much larger quantities, from a few larger components, such as complete bodyshells, produced by outside suppliers. When the production of the Magnette was well under way, Abingdon turned their efforts to the production of the all-new MGA which was launched in 1955. Whilst the MGA was happily furthering the MG tradition, the ZA Magnette saloon was coming to the end of a life during which it had done much the same things, although in a totally different market sector. At the latter end of 1956 the ZA Magnette gave way to the ZB Magnette, with major differences in the power unit. The engine now produced 68 bhp @ 5500 rpm, due to increased compression ratio and

larger SU carburettors. Being capable of over 90 mph the ZB Magnette became the fastest 1.5 litre saloon available in Britain which was endorsed by the fact that it won its class in the BRSCC Saloon Car Championship in 1958. The ZB also displayed several interior detail improvements over its predecessor and was also improved styling-wise with the Varitone model. This employed a two-tone colour scheme and a larger wrap around rear window which apparently was installed by cutting a larger aperture at the Abingdon factory, as the Pressed Steel factory at Cowley, where the Magnette shells were made, never tooled up for this design improvement. A small number of ZB Magnettes were produced with clutchless 'Manumatic' gear changes, which was an early attempt at providing a semi-automatic transmission for the lighter small capacity saloons. Like so many MGs, the Z series had been introduced to howls of initial disappointment, yet proved itself to be a thoroughly capable and much admired car, with over 36,000 examples being produced.

ZB
Varitone Magnette

Specification:

Engine:

Type: In line, water cooled

No of cylinders: 4

Bore/Stroke: 73.025mm x 88.9mm

Capacity: 1489cc

Valve Operation: Pushrod overhead valve.

Carburation: twin semi-downdraught SU.

Power output: ZA: 60 bhp at 4,600 rpm. ZB: 68.4 bhp at 5,250 rpm.

Clutch and Gearbox: Dry clutch and part synchro 4 speed manual gearbox

Suspension: Front: Coil and wishbone

Rear: half elliptic

Wheels: Bolt on disc.

Brakes: Lockheed hydraulic with 10'' drums.

Wheelbase: 8' 6''

Track: 4' 3'' front and rear

Body type: 4 seater saloon

Number Built: ZA: 12,754, ZB: 23,846.

MGA 1500

The introduction of the MGA 1500 was a long awaited event by both the motoring public and the press. The new car before introduction was codenamed EX 182 and was a direct replacement for the MG TF Midget although it was developed from the earlier TD. The car had been finished some two years before it was introduced and existed at that time purely as a design exercise. Three prototypes were built with the code name EX 182 and were officially competition cars, destined to appear at the Le Mans 24 hour race in June 1955. It was originally intended to announce the all-new MG to the public at the beginning of June and then enter three of them at Le Mans, however a delay in the supply of bodies meant that the prototypes had to race rather than production versions. The Le Mans outing proved successful, with the cars carrying a developed version of the new BMC 'B' series engine as introduced on the ZA Magnette saloon endowed with a capacity of 1489 cc. The team met with reasonable results with two cars coming fifth and sixth, the third car driven by Dick Jacobs however crashed in the aftermath of a disaster which killed over eighty people, when a Mercedes left the track ploughing into spectators. Three cars later entered the Ulster TT race, two of which were utilising experimental twin cam engines. Again the results were encouraging, proving the new MGs high speed reliability, which was just what was needed for a successful launch to the new car.

The appeal of the MGA was quite staggering, in the first full year of production in 1956, more than 13,000 cars were built, which far exceeded the entire production achieved over a four year period with the TC. It was evident that MG had come up with the right car at the right time,

with an extremely attractive body, its flowing lines were to become one of todays most desirable classic cars. The 'B' series engine was fitted in standard tune and initially gave 68bhp @ 5500 rpm and later being raised to 72bhp at the same engine speed. The independent coil spring and wishbone front suspension system was directly related to that of the MG TF, whilst the half-elliptic sprung rear axle was that as fitted to the ZA Magnette. It is worth mentioning that several traditional MG features were incorporated from previous models which included lever arm dampers that formed part of the front suspension wishbone layout and twin six volt batteries wired in series mounted either side of the prop shaft behind the seats. The weather equipment was also adopted from previous models being of basic self assembly with separate side screens incorporating flaps to allow hand signalling.

The MGA did however have flashing direction indicators like its predecessor, the TF.

The dashboard too was a welcome return to traditional styling but with a pronounced absence of octagonal instrumentation. The MGA had sensible circular dials, with the rev counter and speedometer placed in direct sight of the driver behind the steering wheel on each side of the column. The fly-off handbrake was mounted on the side of the transmission tunnel, which was effective and ideally placed, likewise the gear change was precise and located in the optimum position for speed of operation. Optional extras included a radio and a fresh air heater, also the car could be ordered with standard steel disc wheels or centre-lock wire wheels. Other desirable extras included a 4.55:1 axle ratio, telescopic steering column and a tonneau cover. A works hardtop was not available immediately but followed a year after the car was introduced.

As indicated before, the MGA was an immediate success, with just over 1000 cars being built before the end of 1955 and in 1956 they were streaming through the factory gates at Abingdon at the rate of 300 a week, in total no less than 58,750 examples were sold with a large percentage finding their way into the American market. This was obviously due to the fact that the car broke new ground in terms of styling, performance and safety, being more civilised and smoother than the TF. After only a year in production, the roadster was joined by a closed-in version, the MGA Coupé. This car was totally different in concept to the open topped car with many refinements found on saloons of the day. Wind-up windows, a wrap-around front windscreen and similar rear screen. Lockable door handles were fitted making the car secure. A total of 100 lbs was the difference between the roadster and the coupe, which meant the car was somewhat slower than the open top version. The coupé was to remain in production throughout the range of ensuing models and was available with all the models including the 1600, Twin Cam and the extremely rare 1600 De Luxe model.

By 1959, time and progress was telling on the MGA. Competitors such as Triumph had introduced disc braking and they also had a weight advantage over the MGA. This no doubt brought about the introduction of the 1600 version with increased power and disc brakes, making 100 mph both possible and safe. The MGA remained in production in various forms right through until 1962 with over 100,000 models having been produced before the introduction of the MGB.

47

MGA

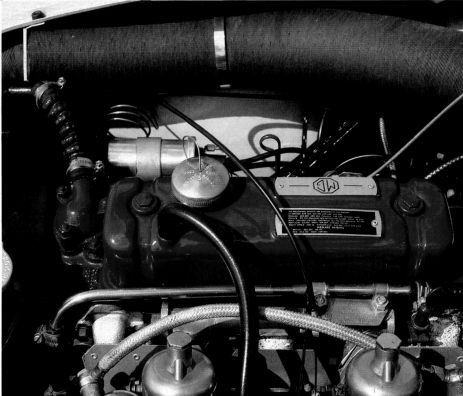

Specification

Engine:
Type: In line water cooled
No of cylinders: 4
Bore/stroke: 73.025 x 88.9mm
Capacity: 1489cc
Compression Ratio: 8.3:1
Valve operation: pushrod overhead valve.
Carburation: Twin semi-downdraught SU.
Power output: Early cars: 68bhp @ 5500rpm
Late cars: 72bhp @ 5500rpm
Maximum torque: 77lb ft @ 3500rpm.
Clutch & Gearbox: Dry clutch, part synchromesh
4 speed manual.
Brakes: Lockheed hydraulic, 10″ drums all round.
Tyres: 5.50-15″ on 4″ rims with steel disc or centre
lock wire wheels.
Suspension: Front; coil springs, wishbones and
lever arm dampers. Rear; live rear axle, half elliptic
leaf springs and lever arm dampers.
Wheelbase: 7′10″
Track: front; 3′0″
Width: 4′9.25″
Price on introduction in 1955: £595
Number built: 58,750
Performance
Maximum speed: 98mph
Acceleration: 0-60: 15.6 secs.
Fuel consumption: approx 27mpg.

MGA 1600

The MG Car Company announced in 1955 that it would again be competing in the Le Mans 24 hour race after a 20 year absence from the grid. The three cars entered were very interesting in as much as they were acknowledged to be prototypes for a long awaited all-new production sports car. Codenamed EX 182, the prototypes returned very creditable performances with two out of the trio crossing the finishing line. With one car coming 12th and the other 17th, (the final car having retired through crash damage) a total distance of 2,084 and 1,961 miles was covered respectively. This impressive result demonstrated that competition was a very worthy aid to development and in fact, apart from a few minor cosmetic and detail improvements, the final production ver-

sion was not strikingly different. Thus was born the TF replacement, the MGA. Production of the TF ended in May 1955 and because of delays in the supply of body panels, serious production of the MGA did not start until September 1955. It was intended to announce the MGA to the public in June of that year, just prior to the Le Mans race, but because of the aforementioned body panel delays, the prototypes took to the track rather than production versions. Tragedy struck at the Le Mans circuit which overshadowed the achievements of the MGs. The third prototype, driven by Dick Jacobs crashed in the aftermath of an horrific incident caused by a Mercedes leaving the track and ploughing into spectators, killing over 80 of the crowd. Adverse publicity following the event caused the MG factory to resume a far lower profile on the competition front, although three cars were later entered in the Ulster TT race, two of which sported experimental twin cam engines. Again the results were most encouraging, proving that the MGs had high speed reliability, it was just what was needed to launch the brand new MGA.
The car made its debut at the Frankfurt Motor Show in September 1955 and was well received by the press and sports car enthusiasts, in fact the buying public endorsed the car to the extent that sales over its 7 year production period exceeded 101,000 units, making it the most popular sports car ever produced up until that time. In the first full year of production alone the MGA production exceeded 13,000 cars which outstripped the entire 4 year production of the very popular TC Midget. It was apparent that MG had come up with a winner at just the right time, with its very attractive flowing body lines it was destined to become one of today's most desirable classic sports cars. Initially the MGA was fitted with the B

series power unit of 1,489 cc that was introduced on the earlier ZA Magnette Saloon. In standard tune, the power output was 68 bhp @ 5,500 rpm, this was later enhanced to 72 bhp at the same engine speed, in a bid to give the car slightly better performance. MGAs were streaming through the Abingdon factory gates at the rate of over 300 per week in 1956 with over 58,000 examples of the 1500 MGA being produced up to May 1959, a large percentage finding their way over the Atlantic to the American market. The popularity was obviously due to the fact that the car broke new ground in terms of styling, performance and safety and was considered much more civilised and smoother that its forerunner the TF Midget.
Within a year of the start of production, the open two seater was joined by a two seater closed coupé version. This car was totally different in concept to the open version and it carried many of the refinements found on the saloons of the day, such as wind-up windows, wrap-around front and rear windows and lockable doors. A weight penalty of 100 lbs was incurred with the coupe body and as a result top speed and acceleration performance was diminished. Nonetheless, the coupé version was popular and remained in production as a variant on the ensuing 1600, 1600 De Luxe and the Twin Cam. It was evident in 1959, after four years in production that the MGA 1500 was in need of some transformation in order to remain attractive to potential customers and induce existing MGA owners to consider replacement.
The high performance 1,588 cc Twin Cam had been introduced a year earlier to satisfy the needs of the more discerning, well-heeled sports car enthusiast, but it was felt that the

1500 MGA could well do with some extra affordable and reliable performance (The twin cam had suffered reliability problems very early on in its production life). Essentially the basic design of the MGA 1600 remained unchanged, however the engine capacity was increased from 1,489 cc to 1,588 cc giving an extra 6 brake horsepower. The marginal 99 cc increase gave a 10% rise in power and a meaningful 17% increase in torque which resulted in a noticeable improvement in acceleration and the top speed was raised past the all-important 100 mph barrier as well. Braking was quite dramatically improved by the introduction of disc brakes at the front and better rear drum brakes, easily coping with the increased potential from the new engine. There were suspension changes on the 1600 with slightly stiffer springs and uprating of the front lever arm shock absorbers but more noticeable were the cosmetic and detail

improvements to the body. First introduced on the Twin Cam, the sliding perspex side windows were a distinct improvement over the celluloid side flaps on the 1500. New lighting regulations dictated an improved front side lamp that incorporated the amber indicator lamp whilst at the rear, separate indicator lamps had to be provided. Chrome plated "1600" badges were fitted adjacent to the front scuttle air vents and below the boot MG badge, to give the uprated car its true identity. Several new accessory options were available on the 1600 that included, headlamp flasher switch, wheel trims, close ratio gearbox, anti-roll bar and battery covers, whilst there were also several new paint and upholstery colour options. 31,501 examples of the MGA 1600 were produced in its two year production span and towards the end of production the 1600 was offered with an intriguing option, which was really a left over from the ending of Twin Cam production. Some Twin Cam chassis were built up with 1600 bodies and drive trains thus allowing the fitment of all-round disc brakes, this variant became known as the 1600 De Luxe or latterly the 1600 Mark 2 De Luxe and it is thought that only 400-500 cars carried the De Luxe badging. MGA production ceased, making way for the MGB, in June 1962 with 101,081 variants being produced altogether.

MGA 1600

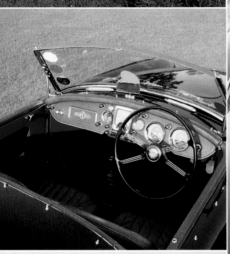

SPECIFICATION

Engine Type: In line water cooled
No of cylinders: 4
Bore & Stroke: 75.4mm x 88.9mm
Capacity: 1,588cc
Compression Ratio: 8.3 : 1
Valve operation: Pushrod overhead valve
Carburation: Twin semi-downdraft SU's
Power output: 79.5 bhp @ 5,600 rpm
Max torque: 87 ft/lb @ 3,800 rpm
Clutch: Single dry plate
Gearbox: Part synchromesh, 4 speed manual
Brakes: Lockheed disc at front, drum at rear
Wheels: Bolt on steel disc, or centre lock wire wheels
Suspension: Front; coil springs, wishbones and hydraulic lever arm dampers. Rear; live axle, half elliptic springs and hydraulic lever arm dampers
Wheelbase: 7' 10"
Track: front; 3' 11.5" Rear;4' 0.75"
Price on introduction in 1959: £940 7s 6d
Number built: (roadster & coupe): 31,501

MGA 1600 MK1 Deluxe

The idea for the MGA was first originated in 1951 when Abingdon's chief designer, Syd Enever was engaged on a one-off project to produce a more streamlined body to fit on the TD Mark II chassis for competition purposes. This was carried out on a car to be driven by George Phillips and Alan Rippon at the Le Mans 24 hour race in 1951. The finished car bearing registration number UMG 400 was easily identifiable as the forerunner to the MGA. With a bulge to accommodate the mildly tuned XPAG engine, the car certainly looked the part and managed to lap the circuit at speeds approaching 120 mph. Unfortunately the car did not fair well in the race and retired with engine failure, but it set the scene for the next generation of MG sports cars. The appearance of the car with its aerodynamic flowing lines, excited everybody who set their eyes upon it, however there was one big drawback with the design in as much as the driver was well exposed to the outside world, with at least half his torso showing above the top door line. This was due to the very high seating position dictated by the use of the TD chassis.

Enever was quite irritated by this as the driver interrupted the whole flow of the car, making the complete package look quite absurd. He therefore set about designing a new frame with its side members well spaced apart so that the driver and passenger could sit lower in the car alongside the transmission line. Two new frames were made up, with one of them being fitted with an almost identical body to UMG 400 and full weather and road equipment which included hood, sidescreens, windscreen and chrome bumpers and overriders. This prototype, completed in 1952, became known as EX 175 but still had a rather unsightly bulge in the bonnet line to accommodate the XPAG engine. When first shown to the powers that be, who included Leonard Lord, the chairman of the newly formed BMC group, there was little enthusiasm shown and in fact it was turned down in favour of following through a tie up with Donald Healey to make Austin Healey sports cars. All that was sanctioned was a "revamped" TD which had a lowered bonnet line, a smaller sloping radiator shell, that for the first time did not actually house the radiator, headlamps faired into the front wings, bucket seats, wire wheel hubs and a tuned version of the TD Mark II engine. This new offering that looked quite different to the TD was designated the TF Midget and it appeared at the 1953 Motor Show priced at only £20 more than the TD. Intended only as a stop gap and really for the overseas markets the TF received a rather lukewarm reception. A year later Lord relented and gave the go ahead for Abingdon to make the replacement for the TF as soon as possible and an announcement was made in time to get the car launched at the Frankfurt, Paris and London Motor Shows in 1955.

The MGA was given an enthusiastic welcome and in its first year of full production in 1956 over 13,000 were built, which exceeded the total number of TCs built in its four year production span! It was boom time for Abingdon with the Z Magnette saloon selling well, total production exceeded 20,000 units and 15,000 of them were exported in that year, which bode very well for the future and demonstrated just how highly MG was regarded throughout the world. It was apparent that MG had come up with a winner at just the right time, with its very attractive flowing body lines, it was destined to become one of today's most desirable classic sports cars. Initially the MGA was fitted with the B series power unit of 1,489 cc, that was introduced on the earlier ZA Magnette Saloon. In standard tune, the power output was 68 bhp @ 5,500 rpm, this was later enhanced to 72 bhp at the same engine speed, in a bid to give the car slightly better performance. MGAs were streaming through the Abingdon factory gates at the rate of over 300 per week in 1956 with over 58,000 examples of the 1500 MGA being produced up to May 1959, a large percentage finding their way over the Atlantic to the American market. The popularity was obviously due to the fact that the car broke new ground in terms of styling, performance and safety and was considered much more civilised and smoother that its forerunner the TF Midget.

From very early on in the planning of the MGA it was decided that the range should include a high performance model. Various proposals were put forward for a twin overhead camshaft engine and the production version of the MGA Twin Cam came to fruition with the announcement of the car in 1958 after a rather lengthy and involved development period. In fact the car returned one of the shortest production runs Abingdon had ever known and with only 2,111 cars manufactured it hardly justified the development costs. Nonetheless the Twin Cam was quite exciting for a 1950s sports car and offered a top speed of 115 mph with braking to match the performance with the fitment of Dunlop disc brakes all round. The standard 1500 MGA continued in production with minor changes until 1959, when the MGA 1600 was introduced which sported a 1588 cc pushrod overhead valve engine and front disc brakes. Very shortly after this in 1960, the Twin Cam ceased production and Abingdon found itself with many surplus Twin Cam components which included, chassis frames, suspension and brake parts and steering racks. It is widely felt that this was the reason that the De Luxe models were introduced in June 1960 to use up otherwise redundant parts and although the cars were originally only built to order, very soon quite large consignments were crossing the Atlantic.

Only 395 De Luxe models were produced in total, which makes the car quite a rarity. Distinguishing features are the Dunlop disc brakes fitted both front and rear and the centre-lock vented pressed steel wheels. Although never referred to initially as a 1600 Mark I, these De Luxe MGA models were available as both an open Tourer or as a closed Coupé. In his book Mighty MGs, Graham Robson quotes from research of the factory records that 70 of the 1600 De Luxe Tourers were built accompanied by only 12 Coupés. The 1600 Mark II De Luxe that sported the 1622 cc engine was produced in greater numbers with 290 Tourers and 23 Coupés being made. Many of the De Luxes were built to slightly different specifications, which highlighted the fact that the "parts bins" were being cleared out, with some cars carrying optional extras as a standard fitment, ie special seats, oil coolers, close ratio gearboxes and different ratio rear axles. With a slump in the American market that hit exports badly in late 1960 and during 1961 many of the De Luxes that had been built in left hand drive form, did not make the Atlantic crossing and were eventually converted back to right hand drive for the home market. One such 1600 Mark I De Luxe that did find its way into American ownership was the concours Iris Blue Roadster featured. The car was re-imported back to the UK and restored to competition winning standard by Chris and Clive Postles, the current owners.

MGA 1600 MK1

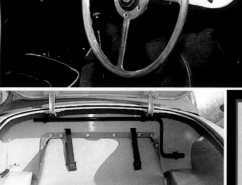

SPECIFICATION

Engine Type: In line water cooled
No of cylinders: 4
Bore & Stroke: 75.4mm x 88.9mm
Capacity: 1,588cc
Compression Ratio: 8.3 : 1
Valve operation: Pushrod overhead valve
Carburation: Twin semi-downdraft SU's
Power output: 79.5 bhp @ 5,600 rpm
Max torque: 87 ft/lb @ 3,800 rpm
Clutch: Single dry plate
Gearbox: Part synchromesh, 4 speed manual
Brakes: Dunlop discs all round
Wheels: Centre lock pressed steel disc
Suspension: Front; coil springs, wishbones and hydraulic lever arm dampers. Rear; live axle, half elliptic springs and hydraulic lever arm dampers
Wheelbase: 7' 10"
Track: front; 3' 11.5" Rear;4' 0.75"
Number built: 70 (Tourer) 12 (Coupé)

MGA Twin Cam

The MGA Twin Cam was announced in 1958 and was the product of a lengthy and involved development but disappointingly it returned one of the shortest production runs that Abingdon had ever seen. This certainly makes the car somewhat a rarity with only 2111 cars being produced between early 1958 and early 1960. The twin cam was to utilise an engine that was never fitted to any other car and was developed from the B series unit, prior to this the PB was the last MG to use an overhead cam engine in 1936. For ease of production, economy and reliability the standard pushrod type of engines were used by MG from then on, but it was evident that performance suffered as a result and it was when the Abingdon engineers became frustrated at trying to extract more than 60 bhp from the B series Austin-derived engine, that was currently powering the MGA and Magnette cars, that attentions were turned to the production of an overhead cam unit. The Company was also keen to get the name of MG back into serious competition, particularly racing, as this had been shelved some years previously during the Nuffield rationalisation.

It was Gerald Palmer who was a design engineer at the Cowley plant who originally set the wheels in motion for a twin cam conversion of the B series engine. In his plans he set the two lines of valves at 90 degrees symmetrically opposed and it was intended that as many of the existing B series engine components as possible should be utilised. The basic designs were then handed over during 1954 to the Morris Engines Division at Coventry to be developed further. It was not until the summer of 1958 that any production units were available for fitting into the MGA and therefore the development work was quite a protracted affair. There was however a prototype twin cam engine which appeared in an MGA that competed in the Dundrod Tourist Trophy Race in Northern Ireland as early as September 1955. At that time there was also another prototype twin cam engine that was under development by the Austin engineers at Longbridge and this too was scheduled to power an MGA in the same race, but due to rev limitations and carburation problems the car never appeared. The Austin unit was a totally new design and not based on any other existing engine with the valves inclined at an angle of 66 degrees it proved to be a very smooth engine that also fitted well into the MGA engine bay. This particular engine however was very short lived and apart from running EX 182 at Le Mans it was never to be seen again. The Morris twin cam was not to achieve any success in Northern Ireland due to mechanical problems although it was considered promising enough to form the basis of a new production car and development was started more or less immediately.

Further development engines appeared in EX 179 and EX 181 record cars during 1956 and 1957 before the final production version was ready in the summer of 1958. These units were, as Gerald Palmer had intended, based on the B series block, albeit with many changes. The unit was bored out from 73.025 mm to 75.4 mm giving a capacity of 1588 cc, this was to take advantage of certain competition regulations, the bores being siamised. The crankshaft had narrowed main bearings and an extended nose to carry the timing chains, whilst the con rods were considerably strengthened. Heavily domed pistons were fitted to these con rods to allow a very high compression ratio of 9.9:1 which meant that the engine had to run on high octane 5 star fuel in order to get the best performance. A special light alloy cross-flow cylinder head carried twin overhead camshafts with valve operation via Coventry Climax style inverted bucket-type tappets. Hemispherical combustion chambers had two valves per cylinder operating at an included angle of 80 degrees. The front of the engine displayed a very complex looking alloy casing which housed the drive gear and duplex chains for the camshafts and distributor. Two smart looking alloy cam covers adorned the top of the cylinder head whilst a large finned aluminium sump helped to keep the lubricating oil cool. The carburation was by $1^{3}/_{4}$" twin SUs with flexibly mounted float chambers and they appeared on the left hand side of the engine as opposed to the right hand side on the standard pushrod engine. New manifolding was produced with separate downpipes for each cylinder making the engine unit look very business like.

At the end of the day the impressive results achieved from all this lengthy development on what was basically a B series block made the exercise worthwhile. A very healthy 108 bhp @ 6700 rpm together with a maximum torque figure of 104 lb ft @ 4500 rpm meant that the new MGA Twin Cam was to be no slouch! There were other obvious changes that were made to the MGA in producing the Twin Cam. The Chassis did differ slightly to that of the 1500 MGA and there were important changes to the brakes and wheels. In view of the 113 mph performance attainable, Dunlop $10^{3}/_{4}$" disc brakes were fitted both front and rear together with Dunlop centre lock disc wheels carrying Dunlop Road Speed tyres. Wire wheels were not available as an option. The brakes were different to any other type of system used on MGs previously and due to the large braking surface area of the discs they were most efficient and did not require servo assistance. One drawback of the system however was the relative inefficiency of the handbrake which worked on the rear discs by means of a separate caliper with small pads and a pivot system that readily seized up without regular maintenance. Externally there were virtually no visible differences in the body compared to that of

the MGA 1500 with both a roadster and a closed coupé being available. It was really only the wheels and the discreet Twin Cam badges that were fixed to the top bonnet surround adjacent to the air intake grille and on the boot lid below the MG Octagon that betrayed its identity. The instrument layout was almost the same as the MGA 1500 but with a tachometer that read 7500 rpm and a speedometer that took account of the top speed of 113 mph. The instrument fascia panel was given a face lift, being tastefully covered in leather, whilst leather was also employed on redesigned, better padded seats of the bucket type. These seats however were only fitted to the roadster as the coupe had a slightly different design that gave more support and were known as 'De Luxe seats'.

Problems with reliability very early on in its production life affected the sales of the Twin Cam quite markedly and despite its sparkling performance the car was regarded as a commercial failure due to its cost, reliability and stiff competition from Triumph in the form of the TR3A and Austin Healey with their 100/6. Both these cars offered better performance and the Triumph was significantly cheaper by some £144. Abingdon's biggest problem was the poor reliability which in the main was caused by the very high compression ratio necessitating perfect ignition timing and the use of top grade fuel. With either not at their optimum, holes could very easily be burnt in the pistons. This coupled with the engine's large appetite for oil caused by chromed rings and chromed bores soon earnt the Twin Cam a bad reputation. These problems were attended to by Abingdon but only just before production ceased in mid 1959. In the short production life of two years only 2,111 examples were produced, 1,801 of which were roadsters. There is no doubt at the time, the Twin Cam was a car that Abingdon was not particularly proud of, but today the car quite rightly has its niche in the MG history book and is a much desired classic.

MGA Twin Cam

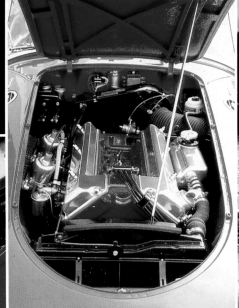

SPECIFICATION

Engine: Four cylinder, in line, cast iron block, alloy head.
Capacity: 1588cc
Bore & Stroke: 75.39mm x 88.9mm
Main bearings: 3
Compression Ratio: 9.9:1 initially, then 8.3:1
Valve gear: Twin overhead camshafts with shim adjusted bucket tappets.
Carburation: Twin semi-downdraught 1¾" SUs
Power output: 108 bhp @ 6,700 rpm
Maximum Torque: 104 lbft @ 4,500 rpm
Transmission: Four speed manual gearbox with synchromesh on 2nd, 3rd and top.
Clutch: Borg and Beck dry plate.
Suspension: Front – independent by coil springs, wishbones and Armstrong lever arm dampers.
Rear – Live rear axle, half elliptic leaf springs. Armstrong lever arm dampers.
Steering: Rack and pinion.
Wheels and tyres: Dunlop pressed steel centre lock disc with 5.90-15 Dunlop cross ply tyres.
Brakes: Dunlop disc brakes front and rear 10.75" diameter discs.
Length: 13'0"
Width: 4'9.25"
Height: 4'2"
Wheelbase: 7'10"
Performance: 0-60 mph; 9.1 secs
Maximum speed: 113 mph
Number built: 2,111 between 1958 and 1960
Price new: Roadster; £843. Coupe; £904

Midget (Gan 2)

In June 1961 the MG Midget was introduced and although not configured Mark I when announced it was for identification purposes dubbed the Midget Mark I. This car was however not an original MG design and was based on the already successful Austin Healey Sprite Mark II. The MG version was promoted as the first MG for 25 years to employ an engine of under 1000 cc and utilised a 948 cc unit. The PB Midget of the mid 30s was the last car to use an engine of under one litre. The Mark I Sprite was unique to Austin Healey and this never appeared as an MG version. More commonly known as the 'Frogeye' Sprite it got its name from the bonnet mounted headlamp pods, giving the appearance of a 'frog' when viewed from the front. This car was introduced in 1957 and when it was announced, there were many enthusiasts who claimed that it should not bear the Healey name and it was seen as a rebuff for MG. To add to this the car was built on the MG production lines at Abingdon.

It is Donald Healey that has to take the credit for the design of the Sprites and Midgets or 'Spridgets' as they are collectively known. He recognised a gap in the small sportscar market left by the demise of the MG TF in 1955 and Healey had already demonstrated in the past that he had the right feel for the British Sports Car market. It was most important to capitalise on this gap in the market and Healey and his design team set to work quickly to design a small sports car to fulfil this need. He was given full dispensation from BMC to carry out this project as their own designers were heavily occupied with the Mini project. There was however very close liaison between the two teams and a ready supply of all the Austin mechanical components that were necessary to complete the project. The finished car loosely resembled a scaled down version of the D type Jaguar that employed a stiff centre structure that enclosed the cockpit and scuttle, with the engine, suspension and steering rack mounted on outriggers at the front.

This type of unitary construction made the car unique and no sports car before had ever been made this way. The strength in the chassis was gained from the sill construction and central transmission tunnel linked into front and rear bulkheads. Additional strength was gained by having no boot aperture, however adequate luggage space was reached through a gap behind the front seats. A one piece bonnet was employed giving excellent access to the engine and all the ancillaries. The 'Frogeye' was to form the basis of a design that was to remain with the Sprites and

Midgets throughout the model's 21 year history. The Mark I Sprite sold very well for nearly three years with 48,960 examples being produced thus indicating how popular this simple sports car was. By 1961 BMC sales and marketing decided that restyling of the body was necessary as many people thought that the 'Frogeye' was too unsophisticated coupled with the fact that the American idea of planned obsolescence was catching on in Britain, hence the Mark II version emerged. It was the result of joint effort between the Healey designers and the Abingdon team under the leadership of Syd Enever. Strangely BMC told Healey to work on the front end of the car whilst the rear end became Abingdon's responsibility with strict instructions that neither camp was to communicate with each other! However with both parties relatively close to each other in terms of distance, collaboration became inevitable. The Sprite Mark II was announced in May 1961 closely followed by the MG version one month later. Mechanically there was little difference from its predecessor except that the engine carried a different camshaft, higher compression ratio pistons and larger valves to give a few extra bhp to compensate for the increased weight. Larger carburettors were also fitted and of the more modern variety, gone were the distinctive brass damper tops to be replaced with plastic ones. A close ratio gearbox was now standard and there was a totally revised dashboard layout but still retained was the now outdated cable drive tachometer which had a take-off from the rear of the dynamo.

The MG version was to be sold through BMC's old Nuffield dealers. Nuffield had been selling MGs and Rileys most admirably in the past and were sports car minded, which helped the sales prospects of the Midget enormously. Both the Sprite and Midget were virtually identical both bodily and mechanically and the only real detectable differences were in the trim and of course the badging. The MG version was to cost more than the Sprite counterpart for marketing reasons and the Midget was adorned with smart chrome strips down the side of the car and a handsome vertical slat grille instead of wire mesh. The interior of the MG was a lot different to that of the Sprite with a seat covering more like that of the MGA which displayed contrasting piping, there was a leatherette covered dashboard with a padded top rail and a plastic white steering wheel. The dashboard layout was the same as the Sprite but for some

strange reason the instrument markings were far more legible. The floor covering was of better quality and that is where the differences ended. The sliding perspex sidescreens were standardised with the Sprite although the Midget could be fitted with a different works hardtop as an optional extra. All this was in line with the BMC policy of badge engineering, thus making the Riley, Wolseley and MG marques, up-market versions of the Austin, Austin Healey and Morris models. Both the Sprite and the Midget were made alongside each other at Abingdon.

Upon introduction the cars were fitted with the slightly uprated 948 cc engine and this gave 46bhp @ 5,500rpm. This allowed a top speed in the upper 80s and a 0-60mph time of 20.2 seconds. The performance was quite acceptable although it was not long before major modifications were introduced. The Morris Minor type engine was fitted from October 1962 onwards. This 1098 cc engine was mated to a vastly improved baulk-ring synchromesh gearbox which was necessitated by the premature failure rate of the previous gearbox. Also at this time an electronic tachometer was fitted and the car now sported front disc brakes and there were other minor modifications carried out. The cars continued to use the existing Mark numbers with the Sprite known as the Mark II and the Midget as a Mark I. After these particular changes the car was sometimes jokingly referred to as the Midget Mark 1½ or more accurately the GAN2 version. The engine change resulted in an increase in bhp to 55 @ 5,500rpm and a torque figure of 61 lb/ft @ 2,500rpm. It was to be 18 months before any further modifications and improvements were introduced on the engine but it was generally felt that the unit was unduly harsh and slightly underpowered. The main changes were in the size of the main bearings to eliminate crankshaft whip problems. Manifolding was modified and larger valves were fitted, together with higher compression pistons. The end result was increased output to 59bhp @ 5,750rpm and a far smoother running engine. These modifications were introduced in March 1964 along with changes in the suspension and the introduction of wind-up windows. Various other changes and additions all added up to a new Mark designation. The Sprite version now became the Mark III and the MG variant was now known as the Mark II. The MG Midget (Mark 1½!) featured is a beautifully restored example belonging to Rod Dunnett.

You can bank on a Midget with safety. And that describes how it corners, hugs firmly to the road, comes docile to a stop – and puts away again to pass in the only safe way with a fast performance through the gears. All world-renowned M.G. features all attributable in a great tradition, to M.G. Abingdon craftsmanship, to B.M.C resources. You start with the best in sports motoring, when you buy a Midget. £472 plus £178.0.3 P.T.

MG MIDGET

MIDGET
(GAN 2)

SPECIFICATION:
Engine: Cast iron head and block.
Number of cylinders: 4
Bore and Stroke: 64.58 mm x 83.72 mm
Capacity: 1098cc
Valve operation: Pushrod overhead valve.
Carburation: Twin semi-downdraught 1¼" SUs
Power output: 55 bhp @ 5,500 rpm
Max Torque: 61 lb/ft @ 2,500 rpm
Gearbox: 4 speed part synchromesh manual.
Clutch: Dry plate.
Suspension: Front: Coil and wishbone with hydraulic lever arm shock absorbers. Rear: Quarter elliptic with hydraulic lever arm shock absorbers.
Brakes: Lockeed hydraulic, disc front, 7" drum rear.
Wheels: Bolt-on pressed steel disc. Wire wheel centre lock option
Wheelbase: 6'8"10⁵/₁₆
Track: 3' front. 3'8¾" rear.
Number built: 9601
Cost New 1963: £495 plus £103.13s.9d. tax.

Discounting the 'modern' MG saloons under the Metro, Maestro and Montego banner, the BMC 1100 based MG saloons were the top selling car in Britain for many years. Over 3 million 1100/1300 variants were produced between 1962 and 1973 with the MG versions proving to be amongst the most popular. The 1100 was quite revolutionary and was described in all the promotional literature as "the most advanced MG of all time!" This statement no doubt raised a few eyebrows from the ranks of the diehard enthusiasts and the car was at the time a most unwelcome piece of badge engineering. Launched at the same time as the all-new MGB, the 1100 was somewhat overshadowed by the long awaited MGA replacement.

Nonetheless the 1100 had its part to play in the success of BMC in the early sixties. Originally there were plans to produce an MG version of the revolutionary Issigonis Mini that was introduced in 1959 that had dominated the small family saloon market for some time. However the Cooper name had become a household name after the specialist racing car manufacturer had won the World Constructors Championship twice and this was capitalised on by a Cooper version of the Mini. John Cooper sold the idea to BMC and both Austin and Morris versions were produced to cash in on the Cooper name. This immediately shelved any ideas of an MG badge engineered high performance Mini. Many design exercises were produced by the Abingdon Drawing Office, some of which were two seater based but sadly the Coopers won the day particularly as the Mini's designer Alec Issigonis did not think that the revolutionary front wheel drive set up was suitable for a sports car. BMC needed however a small saloon car to market alongside the fairly large Magnette saloon which by now was in Farina Mark IV style.

The American market was judged as being ready for an MG 'compact' and with this in mind the badge engineered MG 1100 was launched nearly a year after the first Austin/Morris versions were first seen. Despite the lukewarm welcome the car was an outstanding success from its introduction in September 1962. The MG version was far better appointed throughout, with a twin carburettor engine and a distinctive MG front grille. It was capable of carrying 4 adults with comfort, whereby the Mini would prove cramped. The advanced Hydrolastic fluid suspension provided exceptional ride characteristics and it was the first time that this system had been used on an MG. This new kind of suspension used a water based anti-freeze damping fluid to apply dynamic force to rubber cone spring units. The fluid provided the necessary damping medium to the suspension, thus eliminating the need for shock absorbers altogether. Hydrolastic suspension also removed the pitching problems associated with standard suspension because front and rear units were interconnected. Pitching movements were all but eliminated because shocks to the suspension were instantly smoothed out by an interchange of fluid between front and rear.

The 1098 cc, A Series engine was mounted transversely in the front sub frame and carried an integral gearbox along the same lines as the Mini with drive through the front wheels. A top speed of 88 mph was easily achievable with the engine producing 55 bhp @ 5,500 rpm and with good acceleration to match it was as quick as any of its predecessors. The 1100

was available in two door form initially with 4 door versions following later, it was felt that two doors went better with the sporting MG image! The two door version was to spearhead the attack on the American small car market which in 1962 was dominated by Volkswagen. The MG Sports Sedan as it was known cost £949, however there was a problem identifying which market MG were aiming at with literature and promotional films showing it as an ideal shopping car and at the other extreme, a car suitable for club racing, either way the car sold slowly with nearly 28,000 being sold over a period of 5 years.

By 1967 the 1100 was beginning to look somewhat dated and its initial good performance, economy and handling were being surpassed by competitors. The complete range of 1100 saloons were then given a face lift and uprated. The MG version now sported a 1275 cc engine and the two door body was offered as an option. The fascia and instrumentation was dramatically improved and although initially known as the MG 1275 it was soon adopted as the MG 1300. Four speed automatic transmission was an option but in this case a single SU carburettor was employed. In manual form the engine produced a healthy 70 bhp and the model remained virtually the same until it was

discontinued in 1971 in favour of the Austin 1275 GT, the only changes being in 1969 when the four door option and automatic transmission were dropped. There were other proposed MG versions of the 1100 that never saw full scale production, one being an MG badged Vanden Plas Princess that very soon changed its identity back to Vanden Plas in 1964. The BMC Spanish subsidiary, Authi, did produce an MG 1100 built under licence alongside Minis, they were very similar to their English counterpart except they were left hand drive and carried Spanish instrumentation. A stillborn MG Victoria made an appearance at the Barcelona Motor Show in 1973 but never went on sale to the public, this was similar to a stretched Triumph Dolomite and was adorned with MG badges and a Downton tuned engine. This was to be the last of the MG saloons until the arrival of the MG Metro in 1982. The concours MG 1100 featured is a 1963 model belonging to Ray Shrubb.

soft top—hard ride

hard top—soft ride
thanks to Hydrolastic* suspension

The 1930's were hard times on the road, as elsewhere. The M.G. 18/80 met the demand of enthusiasts for first-class performance and road holding, but it was hard going—literally. Today's descendant the M.G. 1100, with the fabulous fluid suspension and front wheel drive hugs the road even better, but you never notice the bumps. In fact it's an M.G. through and through offering the same appeal to enthusiasts as the 18/80 did 30 years ago. You don't believe it? Then try one today and let it prove itself.

Safety Fast! MG 1100 £100 4 + £139.3.5 PT 4 door de-luxe

THE MOST ADVANCED MG OF ALL TIME
THE MG · 1100
Safety Fast!

955 GYV

MG OWNERS' CLUB

1100

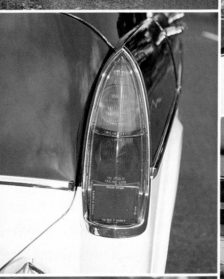

SPECIFICATION:
Engine: 4 cylinder, transversely mounted.
Capacity: 1098cc.
Bore & Stroke: 64.6mm x 83.7mm.
Max torque: 61 lb/ft at 2750 rpm.
Max power: 55 bhp at 5,500 rpm.
Gearbox: 4 speed synchromesh on 2,3 & 4 or automatic.
Brakes: Hydraulic disc at front, 8″ drums at rear.
Wheels: Ventilated pressed steel 4J x 12
Suspension: Front; independent wishbone with Hydrolastic displacers. Rear; independent with trailing arms incorporating Hydrolastic displacers.
Number built: 116,827
Body types: 2 door and 4 door saloon.

Midget MK3 (Gan 4)

When the Mark I MG Midget was introduced in June 1961, it was promoted as the first under 1000 cc MG for 25 years. It was however not an original MG design and was based on the already successful Austin Healey Sprite. The Mark I model of the Sprite though was unique to Austin Healey and never appeared in MG guise. The Mark I Sprite was affectionately dubbed the 'frogeye' due to the bonnet mounted headlamp pods, giving the appearance of a 'frog' viewed from the front. Donald Healey has to take the credit for the Midgets and Sprites or 'Spridgets' as they are known collectively. There was a gap left in the small sports car market after the demise of the TF Midget in 1955 and Healey had demonstrated in the past that he had the right feel for the British sports car market. It was important to capitalise on this gap in the market, so Donald Healey and his team set to work quickly, to design a sports car that would fulfil this need. BMC's own design team were heavily engaged on the Mini project but liaised closely with Healey, supplying him with all the Austin mechanical components he needed.

The end result was a prototype that was virtually a smaller copy of the successful Jaguar D Type with a stiff centre structure, enclosing the cockpit and scuttle, and the engine and front suspension on outriggers at the front. The strength in the monocoque chassis lay in the deep prop shaft tunnel which joined the scuttle pressings at the front and the transverse sloping rear panel just ahead of the axle. Additional strength was obtained by having no boot aperture, however adequate luggage space was reached through a gap at the rear of the seats. A one piece bonnet was employed, giving superb access to most of the steering, brakes and engine components. The 'frogeye' Sprite was to form the basis of a design that was to remain with the Sprites and Midgets throughout the model's 21 year history.

Sales of the Mark I Sprite were very good for some three years but by 1961 BMC Sales and Marketing decided that restyling of the body was necessary. Many people thought that the 'frogeye' was too unsophisticated and the American idea of planned obsolescence was catching on in Britain and so the Mark II Sprite was born. Very shortly after the introduction of the Mark II Sprite an MG version was to appear on the scene being sold through BMC's old Nuffield dealers. Nuffield had been selling MGs and Rileys extremely well in the past and were sports car minded, which helped the sales prospects of the MG Midget Mark I enormously.

The two cars were virtually identical both bodily and mechanically and the only detectable differences were with trim and of course badging. The MG version was to cost more than the Sprite counterpart for marketing reasons and was adorned with chrome strips down the side of the car and a handsome vertical slat grille instead of mesh. This was in line with the BMC policy of 'badge engineering' making the Riley, Wolseley and MG marques up-market versions of the Austin, Austin Healey and Morris models. Both versions were built alongside each other on the Abingdon production line. The MG Midget Mark I was powered by a 948 cc engine and was the first MG to employ an engine of under one litre since the 939 cc PB. Performance was quite acceptable for an engine of this size, the weight savings in the monocoque chassis contributing greatly. 46 bhp @ 5500 rpm was available from the

948 cc unit with twin one and a quarter inch SU carburettors, which gave a top speed in the upper 80s and acceleration to 60mph in 20.2 secs. The Midget was appreciably smaller than the MGA and yet was able to offer reasonable luggage and cockpit space, in fact the rear cockpit shelf could accommodate two extra small passengers if the optional rear seat cushion was employed. Suspension was by wishbones and coil springs at the front and quarter elliptic springs at the rear and a one-piece rear axle.

In 1964 the Mark II MG Midget was introduced with welcome new features, bringing it into line with the specification of the MGB. At the same time the Sprite kept pace with the Mark III version coming on to the market. Engine power was uprated to 59bhp and was enlarged to 1098 cc. The rear suspension was changed to semi-elliptic from quarter-elliptic springs to

help cope with the increased power. The car was also given some styling changes with a new curved windscreen, wind-up side windows incorporating hinged quarter light and lockable doors with external press button door handles. In 1966, a 1275 cc engine was fitted and this coupled with a higher rear axle ratio and an improved folding integral hood became known as the Mark III MG Midget. The power unit offered 65bhp @ 6000rpm, a 0-60mph time of 13 seconds and a top speed of 95mph and was in fact a detuned version of the A series Mini Cooper 'S' engine. The Midget featured is a 1967 Mk III version.

Midget MK III

SPECIFICATION

Engine: BMC Cooper 'S'
Type: In-line, water cooled
No of cylinders: 4
Capacity: 1275 cc
Bore & Stroke: 70.61 mm x 81.28 mm
Valve gear: Pushrod overhead valve
Compression ratio: 8.8:1
Carburation: Twin SU HS2 1¼"
Power Output: 65bhp @ 6,000 rpm
Max torque: 72 lb/ft @ 3,000 rpm
Clutch & gearbox: Dry plate and part synchromesh, 4 speed manual
Suspension: Front; Coil & wishbone
             Rear; Half elliptic
Wheels: Bolt-on disc, centre lock wire wheels (optional)
Brakes: Lockheed hydraulic disc at front, 7" drums rear
Track: Front; 3' 9 ¼". Rear; 3' 8 ¾"
Number built: 13,722
Performance: 0-60 mph; 14.6 secs
Top speed: 93.5 mph
MPG: approx 28.4 mpg
Price new: £684

1300 Mark 2 Saloon

In 1962 a quite revolutionary new saloon was launched by BMC at the same time as the brand new MGB. Initially wearing the Morris badge, ADO16 was hot from the drawing boards of Alec Issigonis and Pininfarina. The Morris 1100 saloon was bristling with new technology and although the Mini had been launched very successfully in 1959, the 1100 was seen as offering quite a lot more for the money. Although similar in layout and concept to the Mini, none of the major components were carried over to the 1100, but in the reverse the Mini was to ultimately benefit from a modified version of the 1100's Hydrolastic suspension arrangement in 1964. As expected, in true BMC style the 1100 became the base for every marque that they owned and whilst it was anticipated that the next model to be released would be the Austin variant in fact it was the MG version that was launched in late 1962. The Austin and Vanden Plas models came on the scene in late 1963 followed some two years later by the Riley and Wolseley offerings. The BMC 1100 based MG saloons were the top selling car in Britain for many years with over 3 million 1100/1300 variants being produced between 1962 and 1973.

The 1100 was quite innovative and was described in all the promotional literature as "the most advanced MG of all time!" Features included, Hydrolastic suspension, transverse engine, front wheel drive, front disc brakes, rack and pinion steering, close ratio gearbox and stylish Pininfarina design. A twin carb 55 bhp A series engine propelled the car to a top speed of 88 mph with good acceleration to match. Launched at the same time as the all-new MGB, the 1100 was somewhat overshadowed by the long awaited MGA replacement, nonetheless the 1100 played its part in the success of BMC during the early sixties.

This civilised saloon was capable of carrying 4 adults in relative comfort and afforded reasonable space, whereby the Mini proved quite cramped. The advanced Hydrolastic fluid suspension provided exceptional ride characteristics and it was the first time that this system had been used on an MG. Mounted on detachable subframes, this new kind of suspension used a water based anti-freeze damping fluid to apply dynamic force to rubber cone spring units. The fluid provided the necessary damping medium to the suspension, thus eliminating the need for shock absorbers altogether. Hydrolastic suspension also eliminated the pitching problems associated with standard suspension because front and rear units were interconnected. Pitching movements were all but removed because shocks to the suspension were instantly smoothed out by an interchange of fluid between front and rear.

The 1100 was available in two door form initially with 4 door versions following later, as it was felt that two doors went better with the sporting MG image! Volkswagen had

dominated the American small car market and this two door version was to spearhead the attack on this lucrative market. The MG Sports Sedan as it was known cost £949, however there was a problem identifying which market MG were aiming at, with literature and promotional films showing it as an ideal shopping car and at the other extreme, a car suitable for club racing. The car retailed steadily with nearly 28,000 being sold over a period of 5 years, but by 1967 the 1100 was beginning to look somewhat dated and its initial good performance, economy and handling were being overtaken by competitors. Shortly after the

Mark II version was introduced in that year, the complete range of 1100 saloons were revised. The MG was given a face lift and uprated ready for the 1968 model year. New rear light clusters, ventilated pressed steel wheels and revised seating also extended into the

Wolseley and Riley variants. The MG version now sported a 1275cc engine and was offered only with a two door body. The fascia and instrumentation was dramatically improved and although initially known as the MG 1275 it was soon adopted as the MG 1300 Mark I. The Mark II 1100 continued to be made and was available alongside the 1300 for a short period priced at £788 7s 9d. Four speed automatic transmission was an option on the new 1300, but in this case a single SU carburettor was used. In manual form the engine produced a healthy 75 bhp and closer ratio four synchromesh gearboxes were fitted to both the MG and Riley versions. The MG 1300 Mark I was available in manual form at £812 19s 5d whilst the automatic version cost £905 3s 2d. The model remained virtually the same until it was discontinued in 1971 in favour of the Austin/Morris 1300 GT, the only changes being in late 1968 when the Mark II version was introduced which adopted the Riley walnut veneer fascia panel that carried a revolution counter, speedometer, fuel, oil pressure and water temperature gauges, A smart leather covered three-spoked alloy steering wheel extended the sporting image whilst optional extras available were an electrically heated rear window and reclining front seats. The pristine 1971 MG 1300 Mk II featured is owned by Maureeen Sawyer

Safety fast!

MG

1300
2 DOOR
SALOON

1300 Mark 2 Saloon

SPECIFICATION

Engine: 4 cylinder, transversely mounted
Capacity: 1275 cc
Bore & Stroke: 70.63mm x 81.33mm
Carburation: Twin semi-downdraught SU's
Power output: 70 bhp @ 6,000 rpm
Gearbox: Four speed, all synchromesh with remote control .
Final drive: Front wheel drive, open shafts with universal constant velocity joints
Steering: Rack & pinion
Brakes: Hydraulic 8.37" discs at front. 8" drums at rear
Wheels: Ventilated pressed steel disc
Suspension: Front; independent wishbone with Hydrolastic displacers. Rear; independent with trailing arms incorporating Hydrolastic displacers
Length: 12ft 2.75"
Height: 4' 4.875"
Width: 5' 0.375"

Farina Magnette MK4

Badge engineering was not a new phenomenon to MG when the Farina styled Magnettes were introduced in 1959. The original MGs of the 1920's were rebadged Morrises and it was the desire of Cecil Kimber who joined Morris Motors in 1921 as Sales Manager, to introduce some special cars with more sporting appeal. Kimber recognised the potential of producing sportier cars based on the standard model range and it was this that prompted the birth of those famous letters MG, standing for Morris Garages, on the sportier, up-market range. The cars generally had more powerful engines, improved suspension, different body styles and more comprehensive instrumentation and this was to be the brief throughout MG history whenever re-badging of models from associated concerns was considered. There have not been many occasions during MG evolution when this practice has been carried out and when it has it has generally been on saloons. There have of course been many saloons produced at Abingdon that were exclusive to MG .

In 1952, the Austin Motor Company merged with the Nuffield Organisation to form the British Motor Corporation and it was at this time that the whole workings of the two companies were rationalised. The merger was seen more as a take over by Austin with Lord Nuffield being retained only in honourary capacity as President. Leonard Lord, Austin's Chairman and Managing Director was in total charge of BMC from the outset and it is known that he personally would have liked to see all the Nuffield marques of Morris, Wolseley, Riley and MG, killed off in favour of Austin. This however would have been a very costly exercise because all the Austin and Nuffield dealers had had such close ties in the past. As there being so many of them, compensation for loss of franchise would have been astronomical, so Lord ingeniously decided to resurrect the badge engineering concept. This meant that BMC would in future produce basic models which could be adapted with different marque badges and trim at very little extra cost.

This was a clever move as it created the impression that the cars were quite different from each other. This worked well with Austin and Morris and other relevant marques but not so well with MG, because in the past the vast majority of models had been unique to MG. In view of the exceptional sales achievements of MG in past years, Lord could not afford to overlook the potential and decided to do the same thing with MG. He did however allow the MG variants to retain more of their own identity compared to other cars in the BMC range.

Thus was born the Magnette saloons with the first appearing in 1953 and designated ZA series. This car was very closely allied to the Wolseley 4/44 which carried the XPAG 1250 cc engine. The ZA was really a replacement for the Y type saloon which had sold very well but become rather outdated. Many purists felt that the MG was a very thinly disguised Wolseley and there were many lively exchanges in the letters columns of the leading motoring journals of the day. "A perversion of the famous name!" was one such comment, but many had forgotten that the very first Magnette saloon was aimed at a very similar type of customer. The ZA however was a resounding success with nearly 37,000 sales to its credit which pleased Abingdon and no doubt the BMC hierarchy. Following closely in

1956 was the ZB series that sported many improvements, not least of which was a healthy increase in power from 60 to 68 bhp. Revised suspension improved the handling and there were one or two trim changes. A 'Varitone' version became available in 1958 that boasted a two-tone colour scheme with colours that did not always go together!. A distinguishing point of reference for the car was the new larger wrap-around rear window, with the aperture apparently being cut out by hand at Abingdon, simply because this modification had not been incorporated on the line at the Pressed Steel Fisher body plant at Cowley where the Magnette shells were manufactured.

Altogether the Z series MGs were excellent cars with a high specification and good performance that few other cars of the era could match. Disappointment prevailed at Abingdon however when BMC decided to axe the very popular ZB in 1958 and this was at a time when it was still selling well although causing problems production wise. Space was at a premium in the small confines of Abingdon and more production capacity had to be turned over to the MGA which was rapidly increasing in popularity. The workforce were further disillusioned when the ZB was replaced by a Pininfarina designed saloon which was basically an Austin Cambridge in sports clothing. Bearing the MG badge and designated the Mark III Magnette it was the first MG to be built outside of Abingdon in nearly thirty years. The 1.5 litre car was assembled at the Morris factory at Cowley where it was built alongside the Morris, Austin, Wolseley and Riley variants. As far as the BMC marketing men were concerned the Magnette was the ideal flagship for the range and they were not unduly worried about the damage this may inflict on the name of MG. It seemed to them by carrying the badge engineering to extremes on so many variants it would give them a short term advantage in the market place and the logic was that by taking an average car it could be sold in larger quantities by investing in the reputation of a good one. There was outrage, not only in the MG camp but also in those followers of Riley and Wolseley who aired their views in the columns of the motoring press about a betrayal of the marque, whilst BMC cheerfully described the car as "Of flawless Pedigree"! Whilst the Magnette was considered a very comfortable family saloon with plenty of room,

good visibility and light steering, its performance and handling were not considered wor-

thy of the MG name, particularly in the 1500 cc Mark III form. Nonetheless the car sold well until it was replaced with the Mark IV version in October 1961. This car carried many detail changes to try and enhance customer appeal. There was improved performance with the bigger 1622 cc engine that produced 68 bhp and gave a marked gain over its predecessor, also changes were made to the steering geometry to improve handling and steering response. For the first time on an MG there was an option for a fully automatic Borg Warner gearbox. A total of nearly 32,000 Mark III and Mark IV Magnettes were produced between 1959 and 1962 when the car was silently phased out having carved its own niche in MG history.

FARINA MAGNETTE Mark IV

SPECIFICATION
Engine: Four cylinder in line
Capacity: 1622cc
Bore & Stroke: 76.2mm x 88.9mm
Valve Operation: Pushrod overhead
Carburation: Twin Semi downdraft SU's.
Power Output: 68 bhp at 5000 rpm.
Clutch: Dry plate.
Gearbox: Part synchromesh manual, with automatic option.
Suspension: Front coil & wishbone with anti roll bar.
              Rear half elliptic with stabiliser.
Wheels: Bolt on pressed steel disc.
Brakes: Girling hydraulic, 9" drums.
Number built: 1961-1968; 13,738

Midget MK3 (Gan 5)

Often referred to as the "Leylandized" MG Midget, the Mark IV version was the first MG to be affected by the rationalisation of the British Motor Corporation. The MG Car Company had up until the formation of the British Leyland Motor Corporation in 1968, been responsible in the main for the design and development work on MGs and this new conglomerate was to strip MG of some of its identity and responsibility. The mergers started back in 1965 when Alvis and Rover got together to be closely followed in the next year by the joining of Jaguar, Daimler and BMC which became British Motor Holdings. Soon after this, the last of the associated companies came into the fold to form British Leyland Motor Corporation which was now to encompass Standard-Triumph-Leyland and the previously merged Alvis-Rover concerns. This rationalisation in 1968 brought together most of the established and well respected British car makers under one roof with pooled resources and expertise second to none. There was a penalty to pay however, with cost conscious accountants making quite dramatic cuts in many areas.

The Leyland conglomerate was headed by Donald Stokes from the Leyland commercial division and it was he who was in complete control of the company. Stokes made no secret of the fact he was not particularly interested in cars, however he was once quoted as saying "Triumph was the only British sportscar" and indeed did not seem to acknowledge that MG even existed!. With the previous takeover of Standard-Triumph by Leyland, MG now were put in the strange situation of being controlled in part by their main rivals, this Abingdon viewed with justifiable scorn. There was tremendous uncertainty about the future of Abingdon and for months after the merger there was very little news about future sports car policies. One thing was

obvious, in as much as Triumph found greater favour than MG at board room level and it was feared that MG could be replaced by Triumph, nonetheless after a short time the two concerns found that they could work in fairly close cooperation and any inter-company rivalries

were soon dispelled. One of the first victims of the imposed cuts was the scaling down of the Competitions Department which was to be lumped in with the newly formed Specialist Car Division. The MG camp were further demoralised by the fact that they seemed excluded from this new venture as it was made up from Triumph, Rover and Jaguar divisions with MG being unceremoniously moved into the Austin-Morris division. The Competitions Department was renamed the Special Tuning Division and still operated from Abingdon, working on just about any Leyland Car, but as Stokes only sanctioned works entries in events that they knew they had some chance of winning, most of the work was on customers vehicles rather than 'works cars'. Sadly in August 1970 the much revered and world renowned Abingdon Competitions Department closed for good with countless successes to its credit, predominantly with MG and Austin Healey.

The Healey badge was to fall victim of these radical changes due to further cost cutting exercises. There was no need to employ independent consultants like Donald Healey to carry out development work, since the mergers of all the different companies had brought together expertise into one large devel-

opment department. British Leyland did however have a contract, originally through BMC, to use the Healey name until the end of December 1970 which was then extended until June 1971 to enable excessive stock to be sold. The 'big' Healey 3000 had already ceased production in late 1967, but the Healey name lived on in the form of the Mark V Sprite and subsequently the Mark IV, but there was to be no Healey version of the 1500 (GAN 6) MG Midget later on. There was an earlier scaling down of the Healey badged "Spridget" when the Mark V was withdrawn from the export markets in September 1969. It was well known that Lord Stokes did not favour continuing badge engineering and with the impending expiry of the Healey contract, this was probably the reason for the decision. Although shortly after this at the October Motor Show the Mark V Healey Sprite was launched alongside an almost identical MG Midget Mark III (GAN 5). With the two cars side by side the only distinguishing features were the different badges externally and in the cockpit, even the recessed grille was the same, as was the selling price of £684. Matt black seemed to be the order of the day, appearing on various components throughout the two cars, such as windscreen surround, sills and the front grille mesh. The matt surround for the screen was short lived and was only a requirement for the Federal US market, reverting back to the matt silver surround when the cars were withdrawn from the export market. New cast alloy wheels, again with matt black centres were fitted and the front and rear bumper bars were of less heavy gauge than its predecessor with the rear bumper split to allow the fitment of a square rear number plate, mainly in a delayed attempt to accommodate American number plates more pleasingly. To comply with European noise level regulations a two piece exhaust system was fitted with the rear silencer straddling the back of the car.

Much to the dismay of the purists the cars were now adorned with British Leyland badges on the sides of the front wings in keeping with BL's policy of de-emphasising individual marque badging. More changes were made for the 1970 model year, with the Healey name being dropped altogether and the Sprite version simply being known as the Austin Sprite and by February of the following year a decision to phase out the car completely was taken. The 1275 cc MG Midget lived on until 1974 with several cosmetic and mechanical changes along the way until the impending American safety and emission regulations got the upper hand. With nearly 80% of Midget production going to the US there was no doubt that it was a popular car and a good earner for Leyland, therefore radical changes had to be introduced to secure its future in the export markets. Thus was born the 1500 (GAN 6) Midget, with an engine unit from the parent company Triumph that powered the Spitfire and huge impact resistant bumpers, the new Midget confidently met the Federal requirements. The featured car is owned by Neil Reynolds.

MIDGET MK III (Gan 5)

SPECIFICATION
Engine: BMC Cooper 'S'
Type: In line water cooled
No of cylinders: 4
Capacity: 1275 cc
Bore & Stroke: 70.61mm x 81.28mm
Valve operation: Pushrod overhead
Compression ratio: 8.8:1
Carburation: Twin SU HS2 1.25"
Power Output: 65 bhp @ 6,000 rpm
Max Torque: 72 lb/ft @ 3,000 rpm
Clutch: Dry plate
Transmission: 4 speed part synchromesh
Suspension: Front; coil and wishbone
Rear; half elliptic springs
Hydraulic lever arm shock absorbers
Brakes: Lockheed hydraulic disc at front,
7" rear drum
Number built: GAN 5; 86,623
Performance: 0-60 mph, 14.6 secs
Top speed: 94 mph
Cost new: £684

Midget 1500 (Gan 6)

The 1500 Midget was introduced in October 1974 and there had been many detail changes to the Midget in previous years to try and over-

come the ever growing American environmental regulations; the 1500 Midget was introduced because it was not possible to modify the existing cars any further. The Midget was completely changed and was not simply adapted as had been done to the previous models with bolting on emission equipment, the fitting of rocker switches, safety handles, and a collapsible steering column. This time the car was radically changed to meet the tough new laws which meant that it would have to be able to survive a 5 mph impact. The cars were put to stringent tests and had to withstand being driven into a concrete block at 5 mph whilst still retaining the functioning of driving lights etc. In addition to this the bumpers had to be set to a regulation height and this was determined by the average height of current American saloon cars. The regulations were treated with some contempt at the time, simply because with all new cars being produced in the States, had to have bumpers at identical height, this meant that all new imports had to meet the regulations. It soon became evident that one fundamental problem was overlooked, in most in-line accidents with one car running into the rear of another, almost invariably the following car under heavy braking would dip its nose and on impact the bumper would ride underneath the rear bumper of the car in front, and at the same time, the rear bumper of the following car would rise upwards on impact leaving it well above the height of any car following that. The end result was extensive insurance claims for badly damaged bodywork due to the immense strength of the new bumpers!

The 'rubber' bumpers as they are more commonly referred to, were made from energy absorbing urethane foam moulded over a hefty steel armature base, they were covered with black polycarbonate which was sufficiently durable to withstand minor scrapes and the ravages of spilt petrol etc. It was not simply a case of bolting on these new energy absorbing bumpers, the whole bodyshell had to be redesigned and reinforced to accommodate them, the existing floor pan was retained to try and minimise costs, however, it was extensively reinforced both to the front and rear. Both the front and rear valances were restyled to accommodate and blend in with the new bumpers. There was quite a weight penalty incurred with all this extra work. This amounted to some 200 lbs in extra weight and as a

direct result of this, the ride height had to be raised by 1 inch in order to stop the car bottoming on the suspension. The alternative would have been to stiffen the suspension but this could not be achieved without sacrificing ride comfort. The ride height was altered by changing the front cross member mountings and recambering the rear springs which now had 6 leaves instead of 5. The end result was a car with quite altered handling characteristics, the extra weight did have one advantage of improving the ride but the changes to the suspension introduced more body roll and made the car altogether less lively. An anti-roll bar was fitted as standard to try and reduce the body movement, nonetheless there was criticism of how the car handled particularly as its predecessors were renowned for their good road holding. At the same time, there was a return to the squared-off rear wheel arches, it was discovered after impact testing that the square wheel arches provided extra strength to withstand body distortion in the event of rear end accidents.

To cope with the extra weight the Midget was in need of an engine with more power, this was achieved by fitting an engine from one of the Midget's old rivals, the Triumph Spitfire. There was no possibility of modifying the already stretched A series engine and it was therefore decided to utilise the 1493 cc Spitfire engine.

This unit was the Triumph equivalent of the BMC A Series and the overall dimensions and weight were about the same, which was not surprising as both engines were of the same 4 cylinder configuration and were both introduced at approximately the same time with the same 803 cubic capacity. The Triumph engine first appeared in the 1953 standard 8, and the BMC A series was fitted into the Austin A30 of the time. The Triumph engine had already been used previously in the Spitfires produced for the American market in 1973, this unit produced 57 bhp @ 5000 rpm and this was with all the emission control equipment fitted. A torque figure of 71 lb/ft was achieved at 3000 rpm, and these figures were similar to those produced by the BMC A series engine of the same period. The export version for the USA was fitted with a single Stromberg carburettor and a reduced compression ratio of 7.5:1. In the home market version the engine was fitted with twin 1½" SU carburettors and had a compression ratio of 9:1. The only modifications needed to fit the engine into the bay of the Midget were a redesigned exhaust manifold and new air intake filters.

With the extra power that was available from the Triumph engine, a wider ratio gearbox was now fitted and was that used in the 1300 Morris Marina saloon. With the new standard gearbox, the extra torque from the engine easily compensated for the extra weight, and reasonable performance figures were returned. Also, a better top speed was achieved mainly due to better aerodynamics and improved bhp. There were other minor changes to the Midget which included the fitting of the Triumph Spitfire steering rack which was slightly lower geared, giving 2.7 turns from lock to lock instead of 2.25. Hazard warning lights, an anti-roll bar and tonneau cover with rail were provided as standard. This more or less completed the package of the car when first introduced. There were then very few changes to the car right up to the end of production in October 1978. However, in January of 1977 head restraints were fitted as standard and in April of that year inertia reel seat belts were also fitted. In the year following a radio console together with two speed wipers and brake failure warning lights were included. The cooling system came in for some modifications because the continually changing emission control regulations resulted in the engine running temperature increasing mainly due to the lower octane fuel. Overheating was experienced and was compounded by the greatly reduced air intake over the rubber bumpers. The only minor modifications were made in September 1977, when the rear axle ratio was changed to 3.72:1 and the Midget also received a door mirror and a 3 part exhaust system to conform to the EEC type approval. The final production modification was the fitting of a dual circuit braking system and this was carried out in October 1978. The very last Midget which was also the last MG to be produced at Abingdon, came off the production line in November 1979.

SPECIFICATION

Engine
Number of Cylinders: 4
Bore and Stroke: 73.7 mm x 87.4 mm
Capacity: 1491 cc
Valve Operation: Pushrod overhead valve
Carburation: 2 1½" SU HS4
Power Output: 65 bhp at 5,500 rpm
Maximum Torque: 77 lb/ft at 3000 rpm

Transmission
Clutch: Dry plate
Gearbox: 4 speed all synchromesh manual

Suspension
Front: Independent suyspension with coil springs and wishbone with lever arm shock absorbers; anti roll bar; live rear axle. Rear: Half elliptic 6 leave springs; lever arm hydraulic shock absorbers.

Brakes
Lockeed hydraulic disc at front drum at rear.
Wheels: Rostyle type with 145 x 13 tyres
Wheelbase: 6'8"
Track: 3'10½" front, 3'9" rear
Length: 11'9"

Performance
Acceleration: 0-60 mph 12.3 seconds
Maximum Speed: 101 mph
Fuel Consumpton: Approx 27.9 mpg
Price new in 1975: £1,559.61

MGB MK1 Roadster

The last MGB rolled off the production line at the Abingdon factory on the 22nd of October 1980 and it ended an era of sports car motoring, not only of the MGB but also of MG sports cars in general. The first MGB to come off the line at Abingdon bearing chassis number G-HN3 101 left the factory in June 1962. The MGB, although launched in 1962, continued in production in similar form, right the way through to the end of its production. During this span of 18 years continuous production, the basic body shape remained the same, apart from the later models sporting impact resistant black bumpers front and rear from 1975 onwards. There were obvious mechanical and cosmetic improvements made to the MGB during its life and these are dealt with in more detail further on. The MGB was conceived as early as 1958 as a replacement for the highly successful MGA and this was before the last of the MGA model range, the MGA 1600, was put into production. There was a design project codenamed EX214 based on an MGA chassis which had quite stunning lines, with the body being produced by the Italian coachbuilders Frua. The overall appearance of this project was quite pleasing and was only marred by the somewhat aggressive front end. This prototype unfortunately never went into production but was the only one produced before the classic MGB shape that was to appear in 1962. After EX214, work began immediately on the MGB project proper, codenamed EX205 by Abingdon and taking four years to develop, it was only anticipated that the MGB would have a production life of seven years!

The MGB was band new car in many respects and was distinguished by its unitary body and chassis structure. It was however not the first British sports car to be built this way, as this type of construction was utilised on the Austin Healey Sprite, Sunbeam Alpine and MG Magnette as early as 1959. The monocoque construction allowed Abingdon engineers to increase the size of the passenger compartment and reduce the overall length of the car compared to that of the MGA. This was achieved by moving the front limits of the compartment forward 6 inches and increasing the width of the cockpit by an inch, all this was made a lot easier without chassis cross members getting in the way. As a result there was far more leg room and luggage space, all in a car that had the same 262 cubic feet as the MGA. The MGB provided a lot more, both in accommodation and performance terms without much of a weight gain over its predecessor. Although the MGB was technically brilliant and had eye catching features, it was a comd-difficult car to produce and the tooling costs were very high. It needed a long production run to recover these costs and as previously mentioned this was projected at seven years, needless to say that these initial costs were recovered many fold.

The basic shape of the MGB was conceived after lengthy development using the EX181 record car as a basis. The very smooth aero-dynamic shape of this 1957 car was used as a reference in wind tunnel tests and had the necessary items such as headlamps, radiator grille and passenger compartment incorporated as smoothly as possible to study the likely effects. Although based around the dimensions for the MGA, the car, as previously described, ended up smaller. The designers incorporated a vertical slat grille, in preference to the sloping type on the MGA, this allowed more room for mounting the radiator and also gave more scope for fitting larger engines at a later date.

Initially two types of engines were included in the design stage, the 1622 cc B series over-head valve engine as used in the 1600 MGA and the 1588 cc twin cam unit. The twin cam idea was very soon dropped and all efforts were concentrated on the pushrod engine. Due to the MGB weighing some 45 lbs heavier than the MGA, it was decided to increase the power of the B series engine as a decrease in performance on the new model was not desirable. The B series engine was stretched by boring out to 80.26mm x 88.9mm giving 95bhp @ 5400rpm and 110 lb/ft of torque @ 3000rpm. However it was not quite so simple as straight boring, for this engine was originally of Austin parentage and first produced in 1947 and was virtually on the limit of its production capacity. All the bores were siamesed except for a marginal water passage between the second and third cylinder barrels. This type of work would have been considered most inadvisable some ten years earlier, but modern casting techniques allowed accurate casting without distortion. New pistons with concave crowns and larger main bearings gave an 8.8:1 compression ratio. The cylinder head, valves, valve gear and manifolding remained unchanged, although larger needles, air cleaners and the exhaust were changed. As a result of the modifications the engine ran hotter, so export models carried an oil cooler fitted ahead of the radiator and it was made available as an option for the home market.

Although the engine had increased in size, the MGB was very similar mechanically to the MGA. The gearbox was almost identical with the same internals, which at this stage did not include synchromesh on first gear, but as it was mounted further forward in relation to the driver, it did not need a gearbox remote extension. The rear axle was virtually the same but had a higher ratio than the MGA. The suspension was recognisable as MGA although there were detailed differences due to the monocoque construction. There were plans to implement all-independent suspension and the EX205 prototype had provision for this type of layout. In the end this configuration was discarded at the drawing stage and conventional leaf springs were fitted. There was a large front cross member, upon which was mounted the entire suspension and steering gear; this was readily detachable from the rest of the car.

Security was an important feature included on the MGB, for the first time an open topped MG had door locks with attractive pull handles and a boot lock, also a lockable glove box and wind-up windows. A comprehensive fascia layout was similar to that of the MGA but there was a neat mounting in the centre of the dashboard for the optional radio with the loudspeaker in the console formed by the bulkhead reinforcement. A fresh air heater was also an option and in 1962 this cost an extra £16. 8s 5d and for a mere £34. 3s 7d you could have wire wheels. The basic price of the MGB when it was released in the Autumn of 1962 was £690 plus £260 car tax. This was very favourably priced against the Triumph TR4 at £750 and £695 for the Sunbeam Alpine. The MGB was only available as an open tourer to start with although within a matter of months a detachable works glass fibre hard top became available. A closed GT version did not follow until Autumn 1965 which proved a very practical, stylish three door hatchback.

Whilst the MGB was in production it seemed that the ageless original design could continue for ever, however there were two projects that were considered as replacements and the first of these was codenamed EX234. It was intended that this car would replace both the Midget and MGB. It was styled by Pininfarina and was conceived in late 1966, being a fairly revolutionary vehicle as far as Abingdon was concerned. Hydrolastic suspension was employed having been successfully tested over a period of time on BMC's front wheel drive Minis and it was thought that a sports car application would suit this system admirably. Internal politics and the need to concentrate efforts on high volume cars meant that this project was abandoned. The second concept for the MGB replacement was worked on in the early seventies and was very futuristic in appearance. ADO 21 as it was known only ever made the clay mock-up stage. It was proposed that this car should be powered by a mid engine and an experimental chassis was made up using a 1750 Maxi engine mated to a highly modified MGB GT shell that carried strut front suspension and a De Dion rear configuration. Unfortunately this design exercise was shelved in favour of those submitted by Triumph for the BL corporate plan for the seventies. The main reason for the decision was the fact that the projected car would have very few components in common with the rest of the BL range and thus would make it an expensive vehicle to produce.

From 1970 onwards there were noticeable styling changes, with the luxury of reclining seats and the addition of pressed steel rostyle wheels, together with a different recessed front grille. In 1973 came more changes with mainly visual improvements to the interior and a distinctive 'honeycomb' front grille. Then in 1975 the most dramatic changes of all took the form of modifications for the American market. These cars had the controversial heavy black polyurethane bumpers fitted front and rear and the ride height was altered to comply with the American regulations. This action did affect the handling quite markedly producing excessive roll on hard cornering, this however was to be rectified in 1976 when a thicker anti-roll bar was fitted virtually eradicating the handling and roadholding difficulties. At the same time as the bumpers were introduced, emission control equipment had to be fitted to the US specification cars, with the end result that the home market cars found themselves with slightly less power. The next significant changes, mainly to the interior, took place in 1977 with a completely restyled fascia that sported a new instrument layout and different control positioning, there was also a new four spoked steering wheel and various other cosmetic and functional improvements. The MGB continued in this form right up to the end of production in October 1980 which is sadly when the last MG rolled off the production line in Abingdon. In those 18 years of production, the basic body shape remained unaltered. It was a design that was ahead of its time and still looks good some 30 years on!

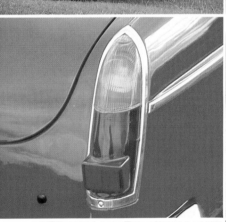

SPECIFICATION

Engine
Number of cylinders: 4
Main bearings: 3
Capacity: 1798cc
Bore and Stroke: 80.26mm x 88.90mm
Valve gear: Overhead
Compression ratio: High: 8.8:1 Low: 8.0:1
Max Power: 94bhp @ 5,500rmp (from 1964 95bhp @ 5,400rpm)
Max Torque: 107lb/ft @ 3,500rpm (from 1964 110lb/ft @ 3000rpm)
Carburation: Twin SU HS4

Transmission
Type: 4 speed, part synchromesh non overdrive
Clutch: Single plate dry, hydraulically operated
Suspension: Front: coil and wishbone. Rear: Live axle with leaf springs.
Dampers: Armstrong lever arm front and rear.
Steering: Rack and pinion.
Brakes: 10.75″ dia front disc. 10″ dia rear drum.
Wheels: 4J x 14 pressed steel (optional wire spoke).
Tyres: 5.60 x 14 tubed crossply.

Performance
0-60mph: 12.1 secs
Top speed: 108.1mph
Fuel consumption: Approx 23mpg

MGC Roadster

Abingdon had been working on developing a bigger and more up market MG ever since the late 1950s with the idea of using narrow angle V4 or V6 engines that were under development at Longbridge. When this idea was dropped a search began for a suitable power unit. The MGB was originally designed to take a 'V' engine of some description so there was plenty of room beneath the bonnet for something bigger than the B series unit. Many possibilities were examined including the light alloy Daimler V8 engines designed by Edward Turner. These engines came in two variants either 2.5 litre with 140 bhp or 4.6 litre with 220 bhp and were well capable of moving the huge and weighty Daimler Majestic saloons at speeds in excess of 120 mph. One shudders to think what may have happened had either of these engines been installed as the MGC power unit! There were rumours of a Coventry Climax engined prototype in V8 form running around Abingdon and at that time, although in early stages of development for other models. There did not seem to be any consideration of the Buick/Rover engine that was later to appear in the MGB GT V8.

Strangely, none of these exciting projects materialised and it was decided to use a modified version of the Austin Healey 3 litre engine although it was deemed unsuitable as it stood. There was also consideration given to an Australian version of BMC's 2,433 cc six cylinder unit, which utilised triple SU carburettors and was basically a development from the 4 cylinder B series engine. This idea was abandoned too because of complicated politics, spares, service and economic problems.

During 1967 BMC and Jaguar merged to form the short-lived British Motor Holdings and the MG Car Company became the MG Division. Because of the continuing rationalisation, there was approval for the production of a new 3 litre saloon known as ADO61, ultimately to appear with an Austin badge. It was because of this that a major redesign of the 3 litre engine was undertaken by Syd Enever and his team and for obvious reasons it was to be this engine that would be fitted to the new MG/Austin Healey sports car and the Austin saloon. It was felt that the engine could be made considerably lighter and smaller particularly with the new casting techniques that had been introduced in the early 60s allowing thinner bore walls etc.

With the 3 litre engine originally weighing in at 611 lbs it was felt that the weight could be reduced to nearer 500 lbs with no problem. In the event the engine, which was built by BMC engine division at Coventry, ended up only 44 lbs lighter and was a mighty 209 lbs heavier than the standard B series engine. Superficially the new engine looked similar to the Healey 3000 engine but it now boasted seven main bearings instead of four, allowing smoother high revving. The carburettors and manifolding were on the nearside of the car with the electrical ancillaries and distributor on the offside. The overall saving on length in the redesigned engine (approximately 1³/₄") allowed the engine to be squeezed into the MGB engine bay, but only just! It was necessary however to modify the bonnet with the now characteristic bulge to accommodate the radiator and an extra small fairing to provide clearance for the front SU carburettor.

The MGC looked superficially like the MGB and certainly shared most of the body panels, chromework, trim and many inner structural members. There were however obvious and important engineering differences to make the

installation of the hefty six cylinder engine possible and changes to the running gear to cope with the extra power. In its final form, the engine developed 145 bhp @ 5,200 rpm and 170 lb/ft of torque @ 3,400 rpm which was a 50% increase over the standard B series engine. There was a brand new full synchromesh gearbox which was shared with the new Mark II MGB that was launched at the same time.

Syd Enever had many problems with the fitting of the engine, particularly as the decision was taken to offer the car with Borg Warner automatic transmission as well. The model 35 automatic gearbox was fairly bulky and theoretically should have been mounted further back in the chassis to give more even weight distribution, but this would have necessitated enlarging the transmission tunnel, modifying the bulkhead and resiting the heater assembly. All of the above would in turn cause the size of the passenger compartment to be reduced which was rejected in the interests of comfort and keeping costs to a minimum. In the end, the weight distribution suffered to the extent of 55.7% in the front and 44.3% in the rear against the MGB's 52.5% front, 47.5% rear. The front suspension had to be redesigned extensively to make room for the engine as the existing MGB cross member fouled the sump. Torsion bars were employed instead of coil springs with anchorages located on the floorpan under the seats, this gave a far firmer suspension than the MGB. Telescopic dampers were used at the front in place of the hydraulic lever arm type because they were able to handle the additional weight that was concentrated over the front axle line. There were only minor changes to the rear suspension but the MGC employed Girling instead of Lockheed brakes which were increased in size at the front to 11" discs and reduced at the rear to 9" x 2¹/₂" drums. Larger 15" wheels were fitted with 5" rims to cope with the car's additional performance potential. The rear axle was of the stronger tubular Salisbury type in common with the latest MGBs and had various ratios at different stages of production and there was the option of Laycock overdrive which was

operative on third and top gears.

When announced in October 1967, the MGC was available in roadster form at £1102 and in GT form at £1249, this was considered very reasonably priced, for one of the fastest production MGs produced. Performance was similar to that of the Healey 3000, but it was delivered very differently, with a top speed of around 120 mph and fast but not dramatic acceleration of 0-60 mph in 10 seconds, the engine showed a lack of low speed torque and refused to rev ferociously and at high speeds was less economical than the Healey. The car as a result received a very lukewarm press reception particularly as some of the press fleet were badly presented at a test session at Silverstone. Some of the criticisms that were levelled in a series of unenthusiastic road tests carried out by the motoring press concerned the gearbox, heavy fuel consumption, general lethargy, heavy steering, enormous steering wheel and probably worst of all, the tendency to understeer due to the increased front end weight. The MGC received probably the harshest reception that any MG had ever experienced and after such comments as 'pig-like understeer' and 'gutless' the points in the car's favour were its refined cruising ability and its comfortable ride and if used as a relaxed high speed tourer, the MGC was a civilised motor car. The high back axle ratio allowed an effortless 100 mph cruising speed at relatively low engine revs of 3750 rpm. One VIP customer worthy of mention was His Royal Highness Prince Charles who took delivery of an MGC Roadster in 1969 shortly before his investiture as the Prince of Wales. The car registered SGY 776F is rumoured to be still in the Royal vehicle fleet at the Royal Mews in London.

After a short two year production, the MGC was withdrawn in September 1969 with a total of 8,999 cars being built; 4,542 were roadsters and 4,457 were in GT form. At the end of production, 200 unsold MGC GTs were purchased by London's largest MG agent, University Motors, and were modified cosmetically. Some had effective Downton engine conversions which gave improved power, torque and fuel economy. These were sold very successfully during 1969 and 1970.

MGC
Roadster

Specification MGC Roadster
Engine
Capacity: 2912cc
Number of cylinders: 6 in line
Bore & Stroke: 83.34mm x 88.9mm
Compression ratio: 9.0:1
Valve Gear: Pushrod overhead valve
Max. Power: 145 bhp at 5,250 rpm
Max. Torque: 170lb/ft at 3,400 rpm
Carburation: twin horizontal 1¾'' SUs type HS6
Clutch & Gearbox: four speed all synchromesh
with single plate Borg & Beck 9'' clutch:. Optional
Laycock overdrive.
Suspension: Independent front by wishbone and
adjustable torsion bar. Anti roll bar and tele-
scopic hydraulic dampers. Rear: live axle, half
elliptic leaf springs and hydraulic lever arm dam-
pers
Brakes: Girling front disc and rear wheel drum
with vacuum servo assistance
Wheels and Tyres: pressed steel disc with five
stud fixing. Optional centre lock wire spoke
wheels. All with 5'' rims
Tyres: 165 HR 15 radial
Dimensions: front track, 4' 2'', rear track; 4'
1.25'', wheelbase 7' 7''
Number built: 1967-1969, Roadster, 4,542. GT,
4,457.
Performance: 0-60 in 10 secs
Top speed: 120 mph
Fuel consumption: approx 19.3 mpg
Price new in 1967: Roadster, £896, GT £1,105.

MGC GT

The arrival of the MGC in 1967 was greeted with mixed reactions both from enthusiasts and the motoring press. It can be described as one of the most controversial sports cars ever produced from Abingdon and during its short life (1967-1969) the car was never short of attention, particularly from the press. The arrival of the MGC was partly due to the flagging sales of the Austin Healey 3000 and the fact that the original design of the MGB monocoque structure was capable of taking larger power units than the 1800 cc engine. It is worth noting however that the MGB suspension, engine bay and general layout were configured for the 1800 cc unit and the idea of fitting heavier, larger and more powerful engines was discounted at first for fear of upsetting the excellent overall balance the car possessed. BMC's policy was not at all clear in the mid 60s in relation to sports cars. There was talk of a modified Austin Healey with different engines and the possibilities of a new joint model badge engineered, but based on the MGB. Alongside this, there was in the planning stage an Austin designed sports car with Hydrolastic suspension and a Rolls Royce engine, which never got off the ground.

It was decided eventually to drop the 'Big' Healey 3000 in favour of an MGB derivative with a similar sized six cylinder engine to the Healey, although technically speaking the only similarity between the Healey and the new MG was in the basic design of the 3 litre engine. BMC were looking at larger engine versions of the MGB as early as 1963 and they wanted to see a car marketed in both MG and Austin Healey forms, in line with their current policy on badge engineering. Both Geoffrey and Donald Healey were engaged to work on the new concept. The two projects were code named ADO 51 for the Healey version of the new derivative and ADO 52 for the MG version. There was to be very little difference between the two cars and prototypes of the Healeys showed only minor changes to the front of the car, mainly to the grille.

The choice of engine was not easily decided. The existing 3 litre unit used in the Healey 3000 was deemed unsuitable as it stood and a refined version of the four cylinder 2.6 litre Austin Healey engine was suggested but promptly rejected. There was also an idea to use an Australian version of BMC's 2,433 cc six cylinder unit, which utilised triple SU carburettors and was basically a development from the four cylinder B series engine. This was not taken up because of too many political, spares/service and economic problems. During 1967 BMC and Jaguar merged to form the short-lived British Motor Holdings and the MG Car Company became the MG Division. Because of the continuing rationalisation there was approval for the production of a new 3 litre saloon known as ADO 61, ultimately to appear with an Austin badge. It was because of this that a major redesign of the 3 litre engine was undertaken by Syd Enever and his team and for obvious reasons it was to be this engine that would be fitted to the new MG/Austin Healey sports car and the Austin saloon. It was felt that the engine could be made considerably lighter and smaller particularly with the new casting techniques that had been introduced in the early 60s allowing thinner bore walls etc. With the 3 litre engine originally weighing in at 611 lbs it was felt that the weight could be reduced to nearer 500 lbs with no problem. In the event the engine which was

built by BMC engine division at Coventry ended up only 44 lbs lighter and was a mighty 209 lbs heavier than the standard 'B' series engine. Superficially the new engine looked similar to the Healey 3000 engine but it now boasted seven main bearings instead of four, allowing smoother high revving. The carburettors and manifolding were on the nearside of the car with the electrical ancillaries and distributor on the offside. The overall saving in length in the redesigned engine (approx. 1 3/4") allowed the engine to be squeezed into the MGB engine bay, but only just! It was necessary however to modify the bonnet with the now characteristic bulge to accommodate the radiator and an extra small fairing to provide clearance for the front SU carburettor.

The announcement of the two models, ADO 51 and ADO 52 was scheduled for the autumn of 1967 at the Motor Show with the original production being sanctioned as early as 1964. Donald Healey was never happy about a badge engineered MGC carrying his illustrious name and it was only after both models had been released for production in the autumn of 1966 that the intended Austin Healey 3000 Mark IV was dropped. BMC tried very hard to persuade Healey to agree to his name being used on ADO 51 and several attempts were made to upgrade the car to a standard that was acceptable, all to no avail. Efforts were then concentrated on ADO 52 with the first true production cars being built in July 1967. The MGC looked similar to the MGB and certainly shared most of the body panels, chromework, trim and many inner structural members. There were however obvious and important engineering differences to make the installation of the hefty six cylinder engine possible and changes to the running gear to cope with the extra power. In its final form the engine developed 145bhp @ 5,200rpm and 170 lb/ft of torque @ 3,400rpm which was a 50% increase over the standard B series engine. There was an all-new full synchromesh gearbox which was shared with the new Mark II MGB that was launched at the same time.

The engineering team led by Syd Enever had many problems with the fitting of the engine, particularly as the decision was taken to offer the car with Borg Warner automatic transmission as well. The model 35 automatic gearbox was fairly bulky and theoretically should have been mounted further back in the chassis to give more even weight distribution, but this would have necessitated enlarging the transmission tunnel, modifying the bulkhead and resiting the heater assembly. This would in turn cause the size of the passenger compartment to be reduced which was rejected in the interests of comfort and keeping costs to a minimum. In the end the weight distribution suffered to the extent of 55.7% in the front and

44.3% in the rear against the MGB's 52.5% front; 47.5% rear. The front suspension had to be redesigned extensively to make room for the engine as the existing MGB cross member fouled the sump. Torsion bars were employed instead of coil springs with anchorages located on the floorpan under the seats, which gave a far firmer suspension than the MGB. Telescopic dampers were used at the front in place of the hydraulic lever arm type because they were able to handle the additional weight that was concentrated over the front axle line. There were only minor changes to the rear suspension but the MGC employed Girling instead of Lockheed brakes which were increased in size at the front to 11 " discs and reduced at the rear to 9" x 2 1/2". Larger 15" wheels were fitted with 5" rims to cope with the car's additional performance potential. A stronger tubular Salisbury type rear axle in common with the latest MGB's had various ratios at different stages of production. An option of Laycock overdrive which was operative on third and top gears completed the package When announced in October 1967 the MGC was available in roadster form at £1,102 and in GT form at £1,249 and was considered very reasonably priced for one of the fastest production MGs produced. The main drawback was in the way that the power was delivered. With a top speed of around 120mph and fast but not dramatic acceleration, the engine showed a lack of low speed torque and refused to rev freely. The car as a result received a very indifferent press reception particularly as some of the press fleet were badly presented. Some of the criticisms that were levelled in a series of unenthusiastic road tests carried out by the motoring press concerned the gearbox, heavy fuel consumption, general lethargy, heavy steering, enormous steering wheel and probably worst of all the tendency to understeer due to the increased front end weight. The MGC received probably the harshest reception that any MG had ever experienced and after such comments as 'pig-like understeer' and 'gutless' the points in the car's favour were its refined cruising ability and its comfortable ride. If used as a relaxed high speed tourer the MGC was a civilised motor car. A two year production span was all the MGC enjoyed before being withdrawn in September 1969 with a total of 8,999 cars being built; 4,542 were roadsters and 4,457 were in GT form. 200 unsold MGC GTs were purchased by London's largest MG agent, University Motors and were modified both cosmetically and some had effective Downton engine conversions which gave improved power, torque and fuel economy. They sold steadily during 1969 and 1970 and are now much sought after.

MG
OWNERS'
CLUB

MG C GT

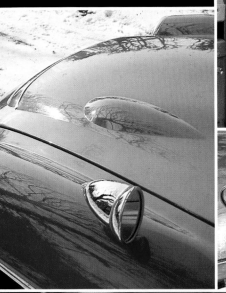

Specification: MGC GT
Engine Capacity: 2912cc
Number of Cylinders: 6 in line
Bore & Stroke: 83.34mm x 88.9mm
Compression ratio: 9.0:1
Valve Gear: Pushrod overhead valve
Max. Power: 145 bhp @ 5,250 rpm
Max. Torque: 170lb/ft @ 3,400 rpm
Carburation: twin horizontal 1¾″ SU's type HS6
Clutch & Gearbox: Four speed all synchromesh with single plate Borg & Beck 9″ clutch. Optional Laycock overdrive.
Suspension: Independent front by wishbone and adjustable torsion bar. Anti roll bar and telescopic hydraulic dampers. Rear; Live axle, half elliptic leaf springs and hydraulic lever arm dampers.
Brakes: Girling front disc and rear wheel drum with vacuum servo assistance.
Wheels and Tyres: Pressed steel disc with five stud fixing. Optional centre lock wire spoke wheels. All with 5″ rims. Tyres; 165 HR 15 radial.
Dimensions: Front track; 4′2″. Rear track; 4′1.25″. Wheelbase 7′7″.
Number Built: 1967-1969. Roadster; 4,542. GT; 4,457
Performance: 0-60 in 10 secs.
Top speed: 120 mph.
Fuel consumption: approx 19.3 mpg.
Price new in 1967. Roadster; £1,102. GT; £1,249

MGB MK3 Roadster

The MGB can rightly be described as the

world's most successful sportscar, with well over half a million cars being produced during its 18 years of continuous production. This figure takes into account all the different mark variants and GT versions and also includes the MGC and V8. The total of 524,470 vehicles can be broken down to individual totals of 387,259 MGBs, 125,621 MGB GTs, 8,999 MGCs (roadsters & GTs) and 2,591 MGB GT V8s. It is hardly surprising that these volumes were produced as the car sold very well throughout its production life and from a design that was conceived as early as 1958 as a replacement for the MGA, its clean uncluttered lines appealed to the masses. Following the MG tradition of affordable sports motoring, the MGB made its debut at the 1962 Motor Show priced at £949 just £7 cheaper than its nearest rival the Sunbeam Alpine which it could easily outrun. The other contender at the time was the Triumph TR4 but although a marginally better performer acceleration wise with its 2.1 litre engine, it had weight penalties and as a result was far less economical than the MGB. The MGB had everything going for it, as it was considered far ahead of its time in appearance and creature comforts and was recognised as being a good performer and excellent value for money. It is true that there were far faster cars around, with the Jaguar E type, Healey 3000 and the Lotus Elan to name but a few and all priced at over £1,200 but the MGB promised an exceptional package for the money.

The MGB was not the first MG production car to utilise monocoque construction techniques. Other BMC products in the shape of the Austin Healey Sprite and the MG Magnette saloon had already paved the way as early as 1959. One of the briefs to the design team was to ensure that the MGA successor had more accommodation and the relatively new unitary construction methods allowed Abingdon engineers to increase the size of the passenger compartment without compromising the overall dimensions. The basic shape of the MGB was conceived after lengthy development work on the EX 181 record car. This 250 mph teardrop-shaped record breaker featured heavily in Syd Enever's design studies and although the end product did not resemble EX 181 in appearance, many of the lessons learnt from this record project were applied both aerodynamically and mechanically. The MGB provided considerably more space for its occupants and the luggage carrying capacity was also improved, all in a vehicle that was some 3 inches shorter than the MGA both in wheelbase and length. The MGB was two inches wider and no taller than the MGA and yet shared the same 262 cubic feet. A weight penalty of just under 100 lbs was more than

made up for in the increased output from the B series 1798 cc engine which was achieved with a change to HS4 carburettors and new Cooper paper element intake filters. The bore and stroke were also revised as was the compression ratio which gave a nett gain overall of 3bhp.

Whilst the MGB was in production, it seemed that the ageless original design could remain in production for ever and although the basic shape remained the same from 1962 to 1980 in the intervening years there were many modifications, some major, some minor. Most of the production changes were cosmetic but some centered on mechanical improvement. There is no clearly defined designation for the MGB and a lot of the changes did not necessarily combine with a mark change. The original mark nomenclature fell by the wayside in the mid sixties and was finally abandoned after the British Leyland takeover in 1968. The Mark I MGB started the series in late 1962 and was followed by the Mark II version in late 1967 which carried through to late 1969 when a major facelift was announced. This model was the first of the new Leyland breed and coincided with the absorption of MG into the Austin Morris division of British Leyland.

The revamped MGB carried no Mark designation at all, but with the passage of time has assumed the Mark III designation. Sales of the MGB continued to be very good and whilst these changes for the 1970 model year were largely cosmetic, it had been projected that the late sixties would probably see the end of the useful production life of the MGB. Tooling costs had been easily recovered, but lack of investment in MG with more favour being shown towards Triumph meant that the MGB would remain in active production for at least another decade. Cosmetic changes were often employed to renew interest in flagging sales but this was not necessary for the evergreen MGB at this time, although BL obviously thought it was. The changes for 1970 model year were carried out both inside and outside the car. Externally the new corporate identity of BL was thrust upon Abingdon by the Longbridge designers, small BL badges adorned the front wings and out at a stroke went the very popular vertical slat chrome grille, to be replaced by a less inspiring, sombre black recessed variety. A new introduction was the replacement of the pressed steel disc wheels with the smarter Rostyle pressed steel wheels. The option of wire spoke wheels was retained and remained a very popular optional extra, whilst inside the cockpit, new PVC reclining seats with optional headrests improved creature comfort. A smart new three spoked leather rimmed steering wheel necessitated the moving of the horn push to a column mounted stalk and a dipping rear view mirror, completed the first of several cosmetic facelifts that the MGB was to undergo over the period 1969 to 1971.

A year later the overriders front and rear carried black rubber inserts to absorb very minor parking nudges and the bonnet and boot rod stays were replaced with more practical telescopic self locking stays. At this time a better folding hood designed by Michelotti was introduced on the Roadster and an improved heater was welcomed. Within the next twelve months, yet more improvements were introduced in readiness for the 1972 model year. These centered mainly on the interior and were intended to portray a more comfortable

impression to intending purchasers. A new

centre console housed the radio aperture and carried the interior light. Neater rocker switches replaced the old toggle switches and a new padded centre arm rest lifted to reveal a small storage area for odds and ends. The moving of the radio to the centre console allowed for the introduction of adjustable fresh air vents accommodated in the old radio aperture in the centre of the dashboard. A welcome safety improvement was the fitting of the collapsible steering column that had been mandatory on the 1967 US specification cars. The unpopular recessed black grille survived only until October 1972 when it was replaced by a new 'honeycomb' type that resorted to the old chrome surround and a central vertical chrome bar that carried the traditional MG shield badge. The MGB was to see several other cosmetic changes, including the controversial impact absorbing bumpers, before production finally ended in 1980 coinciding with the closure of Abingdon.

MGB MK3 ROADSTER

SPECIFICATION

Engine

No of cylinders: 4

Valve operation: Overhead operated by pushrods

o of bearings: 5 main

Bore & stroke: 80.26mm x 88.9mm

Capacity: 1,798 cc

Power output: 95 bhp at 5,400 rpm

Max torque: 110 lb/ft at 3,000 rpm

Compression ratio: 8.8:1

Carburation: Twin SU HS4

Transmission: 4 forward speed, 1 reverse all synchromesh

Clutch: Single dry plate

Suspension: Front; independent coil & wishbone Rear; live axle with leaf springs

Dampers: Armstrong lever arm front & rear

Steering: Rack and pinion

Brakes: Hydraulic with servo assistance, Front; 10.75" dia drum Rear;10.00" dia drum

Acceleration: 0-60 mph; 11.00 secs Maximum speed: 105.0 mph

MGB GT

When launched in May 1962, the MGB was to become for many, the epitome of the modern British sportscar; who would have thought that this MG model with its stunning lines would prove to be the last MG to be built at the famous Abingdon factory. The MGB was in continuous production up until the closure of Abingdon in October 1980 and throughout its 18 year life span the basic body shape remained unaltered. This was apart from the post 1975 models sporting impact resistant black bumpers front and rear, primarily to meet the American safety legislation. The affordable MGB spawned many variants along the way and this was from a car that was mainly intended to be a two seater replacement for the hugely successful MGA. The GT version was announced in October 1965 and was an overnight success, again it was an affordable and very practical car that could carry two additional (although small framed) passengers in the rear compartment. The rear seat back could be folded to give a large luggage platform which was accessed from the stylish rear tailgate.

The original concept of the two seater open sports MGB was considered ahead of its time in 1962 and still had not dated after production ceased in 1980 when the last MGB rolled off the Abingdon assembly line. Over half a million examples of the car in its various guises were produced, making it the best selling MG of all time. In addition to the Pininfarina styled MGB GT more powerful variants were introduced starting with the much maligned 3 litre, 6 cylinder MGC in October 1967 which also appeared in GT style. Later in August 1973 the MGB GT V8 was launched which sadly never saw the light of day in roadster form and was a low volume production of only 2591 cars. There were two limited production runs which both have their niche in MG history, commencing with the Anniversary MGB GT, a limited edition run of 750 cars to celebrate 50 years of MG production. These green with gold livery GTs were launched in May 1975 and are now very much sought after as collectors cars. To mark the end of MGB production and sadly the last MGs to be produced at the Abingdon factory, a limited run of 1000 cars were built in distinctive metallic paintwork. Known as the Limited Edition, 580 GTs in Pewter Grey and 420 Roadsters in Bronze were completed by a demoralised workforce.

The GT version of the MGB was a high priority for Abingdon, in fact it is known that John Thornley and Syd Enever would dearly have liked to produce this car prior to the open topped MGB, but mindful of the public demand for the MGA replacement the roadster won the

day. Within three years of the launch of the MGB, the GT made its debut at the 1965 Earls Court Motor Show. It was evident that the public would have liked more refinement as far back as the introduction of the MGA roadster in 1955, because there was high demand for factory hardtops for these cars. In 1956 a coupé version of the MGA was announced but this still did not afford any extra cabin space and it was to be another 9 years until the arrival of the MGB GT before proper provision was made for the comfort of the occupants and a sensible load carrying capacity. The Abingdon designers were mindful of public demand for greater refinement in their sports cars. Many potential customers were calling for a car that looked a true sports car on

the one hand but carried many of the creature comforts normally only found on the more staid saloon cars. The MGA coupé fitted the bill to a degree with wind up windows, lockable doors etc but it was not until the advent of the MGB GT that the more discerning sports car owners' dreams were realised.

A forerunner to the GT appeared in January 1964 albeit not a factory produced version. Jaques Coune, a Belgian coachbuilder designed and built the Berlinette MGB 1800 which many people believed was the prototype on which the factory GT was based. In fact it was produced totally independently of Abingdon although it was the Managing Director of the Nuffield Press who commissioned the first car and whilst the car received the nod of approval from some of the BMC hierarchy, the connection went no further than that. Whilst Coune had produced a vehicle that was loosely similar to the GT that was still on the drawing board in Abingdon, the Berlinette was made in such small numbers (58 in total) that it in no way detracted from the factory project. 20 months later the MGB GT was launched to a very enthusiastic motoring press and with glowing reports in every journal, the car was assured immediate success. On sale at £825 plus purchase tax of £173 8s 9d the GT was exceptional value and the total price was just under the £1000 psychological barrier. This however was the just for the basic car, many of the refinements were listed as optional extras, such as £14 6s 1d for a fresh air heater, overdrive was an option at £60 8s 4d whilst seat belts (not compulsory in 1965 were £3 5s 0d each!

The MGB when launched was an all-new car in many respects and was distinguished by its unitary body and chassis structure. This monocoque construction allowed engineers more scope with design and layout of the passenger compartment particularly with the absence of intrusive cross members that were so evident on the forerunners. The GT version gave considerably more accommodation than the Roadster with the occasional rear seat and the very usable luggage platform. Weighing in at 251 lbs heavier than the Roadster, the GT was not such a good performer acceleration wise as the open top version, although due to the GTs superior aerodynamics a higher top speed of over 100 mph was achievable. The Italian design studio of Pininfarina were responsible for the GTs very pleasing lines and it was one of the first mass production cars to benefit from the relatively newly developed computer aided design techniques. Many Roadster components were common to the GT, although it carried some that were unique, such as the doors, wings and obviously the roof. Mechanically it was virtually identical to the Roadster with the exception of the fitment of a Salisbury type tube axle, different spring ratings. The new five bearing engine introduced on the Roadster in 1964 was fitted on the GT from inception. In its 15 year production span the GT was to prove a very popular and adaptable car with over 125,000 examples built. Ultimately through lack of investment, forced legislation, economic pressures and too many top Leyland management showing unjustified support for the development of Triumph, the MGB and GT together with the Midget were killed off and assigned to the history books and with them the famous Abingdon factory. The concours MGB GT featured is owned by Peter Morgan.

MGB GT

SPECIFICATION
Engine: 4 cylinder in line
Capacity: 1,798cc
Bore & Stroke: 80.26mm x 88.9mm
Valve operation: overhead operated by tappets,
pushrods and rockers.
No of bearings: 5 main
Power output: 97 bhp at 5,500 rpm
Maximum torque: 105lb/ft at 2,500 rpm
Compression ratio: 9.0:1
Carburation: Twin SU's
Clutch: Single dry plate
Suspension: front; coil and wishbone. rear; live
axle with semi elliptic leaf springs.
Dampers: Armstrong lever arm front & rear
Steering: Rack and pinion
Brakes: Hydraulic with servo assistance. Front;
10.75" dia disc.
Rear; 10" dia drum
Maximum speed: 104 mph
Acceleration: 0-60 mph: 13.0 secs
Fuel consumption: 25 mpg.

MGB GT Anniversary

In May 1975 Abingdon produced 750 specially prepared MGB GTs to celebrate what British Leyland thought to be the MG Car Company's fiftieth anniversary of the production of MG Cars. However as MG historian Wilson McComb points out in his book 'MG by McComb' they got the date wrong as they were actually in their fifty second year of production!

These cars were based on the 'black bumpered' MGB GTs introduced in December 1974 to conform to the requirements of the American safety standards. MG were the first British manufacturers to produce a vehicle to meet the new Federal US regulations on impact absorbing bumpers and exhaust emission control. These regulations stipulated that a 5 mph impact should cause no damage to the safety related systems such as lights, brakes, steering etc. The Californian State regulations were even more stringent and as this was the prime market for MG there was no alternative but to comply. The Californian regulations stipulated that no damage whatsoever should be caused in the event of a 5 mph impact. The result of these regulations meant that substantial steel beams were fitted to the front and rear of the car braced by stiffening struts incorporated into the body structure. Mounted onto this massive framework were black moulded polyurethane bumpers, which were designed to absorb the effects of a 5 mph impact and then recover their normal shape afterwards. In many enthusiasts eyes this ridiculed the classic lines of the GT and to add insult to injury the ride height had to be raised by 1½" to make the bumpers effective. This not only lessened the car's sporting appeal but also adversely affected the handling by producing a lot of body roll and oversteer. Coupled with the fact that the car was now some 70 lbs heavier and 5" longer, it was not as desirable initially as its predecessor the 'chrome bumpered' MGB. This was a classic case of legislators concentrating their efforts on reducing the risks of personal injury at the expense of making the vehicle more accident prone.

In the process of adhering to the American regulations that had spoilt appearance and roadholding, the performance was also markedly affected with air pollution controls becoming a lot more stringent. The North American specification MGBs were detuned with a reversion to the original small valve cylinder head and a single Zenith Stromberg carburettor in place of the twin SUs, together with a highly restrictive air cleaner that made the car particularly sluggish. In addition to all

this, the Californian specification cars were fitted with a catalytic converter to reduce the levels of carbon monoxide emitted into the atmosphere. The Californian Authorities as always were further advanced than the rest of the States with their pollution requirements and as a result the MGB had to carry additional weight and a power loss of some 25bhp. Non-American models were spared the indignity of the drastic engine strangulation, but the other suspension and body changes were implemented to keep production costs down.

Further changes to the MGB and GT brought them into line with the MGB GT V8 with the fitting of a collapsible steering column together with corresponding column mounted stalk controls and V8 type instrumentation incorporating smaller tachometer and speedometer. Door mirrors, hazard warning lights and brake servo became standard fitments and the previously optional Laycock D type overdrive with its 3.13 overall ratio was changed to the later LH unit, with a 3.2 overall ratio becoming standard in June 1975. Twin 6 volt batteries were abandoned in favour of a single heavy duty 12 volt battery but it was still mounted in the well behind the front seats. Moves were made to improve the roadholding in the summer of 1976 due to a high level of complaints resulting from the increased ride height. This was effected by fitting a rear anti-roll bar and a larger diameter one at the front. This did improve things considerably but some fast drivers found that they could lift a rear wheel on hard cornering. The fitting of the new rear anti roll bar meant that the fuel tank had to be redesigned to accommodate it, this made the tank smaller thus reducing its capacity by approximately one gallon. Several other significant changes carried out at the same time involved the part redesign of the interior taking account of some of the niggling problems never rectified during the 14 years of production. This involved moving the overdrive switch to a gear lever mounted position for ease of operation and the brake, clutch and accelera-

tor pedals were remounted to make proper

heeling and toeing possible. A smaller 15" diameter PVC covered steering wheel was fitted, with padded spokes making an 'H' pattern conforming to safety regulations, at the same time the steering rack ratio was increased from 3.5 turns lock to lock to 3.0 turns to compensate. The dashboard was changed extensively having a new non-lockable glove box and all the switches were illuminated internally. A new centre console housed an electric clock together with two new controls for the two speed heater. All cars were now built in the discontinued MGB GT V8 body shell with a forward mounted cross flow radiator and a thermostatically controlled electric cooling fan, which was much quieter than the earlier belt driven fan. Halogen headlights became standard as did all round tinted glass and head restraints. The colour schemes and choice of material for the seats although fashionable were somewhat overpowering and resembled striped deck chair canvas.

The MGB GT Anniversary model was announced in the summer of 1975 to celebrate British Leyland's own interpretation of the 50th Anniversary of the start of MG production. They were all in GT form and finished in British Racing Green with a distinctive gold stripe running the length of the car. There was a commemorative symbol in the form of an MG Octagon on the front wing above and ahead of the corporate British Leyland badge depicting production from 1925 to 1975. Mechanically the cars were all standard four cylinder models but they were fitted with special V8 type steel and alloy wheels painted gold with a black centre cap sporting a gold MG motif. Larger 175 section tyres were fitted together with head restraints, overdrive and tinted glass. A deviation from the normal GT was the colour keyed British Racing Green waist rail trim and black wing mirror housings. The original purchaser was supplied by the dealer with a commemorative dashboard plaque showing the production number from the 750 limited run. It has been said that one car was produced for each of the British Leyland UK franchises that existed in 1975 and research has shown that this could be true. Pam and John Hall are the owners of the featured car.

MGB GT
Anniversary Model

Specification:

Engine
No of cylinders: 4 in line
Main bearings: 5
Capacity: 1798 cc
Bore & stroke: 80.26mm x 88.90mm
Valve gear: Overhead
Compression ratio: 9.0:1
Carburation: Twin SU HIF4
Max Power: 84 bhp @ 5,500 rpm
Max torque: 105 lb ft @ 2,500 rpm

Transmission
Type: 4 speed all synchromesh. Overdrive of 3rd and top.

Suspension:
Front: Double wishbone with coil springs and anti roll bar
Dampers: Hydraulic lever arm
Rear: Live axle with leaf springs
Dampers: Hydraulic lever arm
Steering: Rack and pinion
Brakes: 10.75″ dia disc front; 10′ dia drum rear with servo assistance.
Wheels: Alloy and steel 175 x 14 on 5″ rims

Performance
0-60 mph: 14.0 secs
Top speed: 104 mph
Consumption: approx 26 mpg
Number built: 750 (car featured is number 410)

MGB (Post 1975)

Although launched in late 1962, the MGB continued in production in similar form, right the way through to October 1980. During this span of 18 years continuous production, the basic body shape remained the same, apart from the later models sporting impact resistant black bumpers front and rear from 1975 onwards. There were obvious mechanical and cosmetic improvements made to the MGB during its life and these will be dealt with in more detail further on. The MGB was conceived as early as 1958 as a replacement for the highly successful MGA and this was before the last of the MGA model range, the MGA 1600 was put into production. There was a design project codenamed EX 214 based on an MGA chassis which had quite stunning lines, with the body being produced by the Italian coachbuilders Frua. The overall appearance of this project was quite pleasing and was only marred by the somewhat aggressive front end. This prototype unfortunately never went into production but was the only one produced before the classic MGB shape that was to appear in 1962. After EX214, work began immediately on the MGB project proper, codenamed EX205 by Abingdon and taking four years to develop, it was only anticipated that the MGB would have a production life of seven years!

The MGB was an all new car in many respects and was distinguished by its unitary body and chassis structure. It was however not the first British sports car to be built this way, as this type of construction was utilised on the Austin Healey Sprite, Sunbeam Alpine and MG Magnette as early as 1959. The monocoque construction allowed Abingdon engineers to expand the size of the passenger compartment and reduce its length and decrease the overall length of the car compared to that of the MGA. This was achieved by moving the front limits of the compartment forward 6 inches and increasing the width of the cockpit by an inch, all this was made a lot easier without the hinderance of chassis cross members. As a result there was far more leg room and luggage space, all in a car that shared the same 262 cubic feet as the MGA. The MGB provided a lot more, both in accommodation and performance terms without much of a weight gain over its predecessor. Although the MGB was technically brilliant and had eye catching features, it was a complicated car to produce and the tooling costs were very high. It needed a long production run to recover these costs and as previously mentioned this was projected as

seven years, needless to say that these initial costs have been recovered over and over again.

The basic shape of the MGB was conceived after lengthy development using the EX181 record car as a basis. The very smooth aerodynamic shape of this 1957 car was used as a reference in wind tunnel tests and had the necessary items such as headlamps, radiator grille and passenger compartment incorporated as smoothly as possible to study the likely effects. Although based around the dimensions of the MGA, the car, as previously described, ended up smaller. The designers incorporated a vertical slat grille, in preference to the sloping type on the MGA, this allowed more room for mounting the radiator and also gave more scope for fitting larger engines at a later date.

Initially, two types of engines were included in the design stage, the 1622 cc B series overhead valve engine as used in the 1600 MGA and the 1588 cc twin cam unit. The twin cam idea was very soon dropped and all efforts were concentrated on the pushrod engine. Due to the MGB weighing some 45 lbs heavier than the MGA, it was decided to increase the power of the B series engine as a decrease in performance on the new model was not desirable. The B series engine was stretched by boring out to 80.26mm x 88.9mm giving 95 bhp @ 5400 rpm and 110 lb/ ft of torque @ 3000 rpm. However it was not quite so simple as straight boring, for this engine was originally of Austin parentage and first produced in 1947 and was virtually on the limit of its production capacity. All the bores were siamesed except for a marginal water passage between the second and third cylinder barrels. This type of work would have been considered most inadvisable some ten years earlier, but modern casting techniques allowed accurate casting without distortion. New pistons with concave crowns and larger main bearings, gave an 8.8:1 compression ratio. The cylinder head, valves, valve gear and manifolding remained

unchanged, although larger needles, air cleaners and the exhaust were changed. As a result of the modifications the engine ran hotter, so export models were fitted with an oil cooler ahead of the radiator and it was made available as an option for the home market.

Although the engine had increased in size, the MGB was very similar mechanically to the MGA. The gearbox was almost identical with the same internals, which at this stage did not include synchromesh on first gear, but as it was mounted further forward in relation to the driver, it did not need a gearbox remote extension. The rear axle was virtually the same but had a higher ratio than the MGA. The suspen-

sion was recognisable as MGA although there were detailed differences due to the monocoque construction. There were plans to implement all-independent suspension and the EX205 prototype had provision for this type of layout. In the end this configuration was discarded at the drawing stage and conventional leaf springs were fitted. There was a large front cross member, upon which was mounted the entire suspension and steering gear; this was readily detachable from the rest of the car Security was an important feature included on the MGB, for the first time an open topped MG had door and boot locks, a lockable glove box and wind up windows. A comprehensive fascia layout was similar to that of the MGA but there was a neat mounting in the centre of the dashboard for the optional radio with the loudspeaker in the console formed by the bulkhead reinforcement. A fresh air heater was also an option and in 1962 this cost an extra £16 8s 5d and for a mere £34 3s 7d you could have wire wheels. The basic price of the MGB when it was released in the Autumn of 1962 was £690 plus £260 car tax. This was very favourably priced against the Triumph TR4 at £750 and £695 for the Sunbeam Alpine. The MGB was only available as an open tourer to start with although within a matter of months a detachable works glass fibre hard top became available. A closed GT version did not follow until Autumn 1965 which proved a very practical, stylish three door hatchback.

From 1970 onwards there were noticeable styling changes, with the luxury of reclining seats and the addition of pressed steel Rostyle wheels, together with a different recessed front grille. In 1973 came more changes with mainly visual improvements to the interior and a distinctive 'honeycomb' front grille. Then in 1975 the most dramatic changes of all took the form of modifications for the American market. These cars had the controversial heavy black polyurethane bumpers fitted front and rear and the ride height was altered to comply with the American regulations. This action did affect the handling quite markedly producing excessive roll on hard cornering, this however was to be rectified in 1976 when a thicker anti-roll bar was fitted virtually eradicating the handling and roadholding difficulties.

At the same time as the bumpers were introduced, emission control equipment had to be fitted to the US specification cars, with the end result that the home market cars found themselves with slightly less power. The next significant changes, mainly to the interior, took place in 1977 with a completely restyled fascia that sported a new instrument layout and different control positioning, there was also a new four spoked steering wheel and various other cosmetic and functional improvements. The MGB continued in this form right up to the end of production in October 1980, which is sadly when the last MG rolled off the production line in Abingdon. In those 18 years of production, the basic body shape stayed the same, a timeless design that remains a very attractive and desirable classic car.

MGB

Specification 1962 MGB
Engine
Number of cylinders: 4
Main bearings: 3
Capacity: 1798cc
Bore and Stroke: 80.26mm x 88.90mm
Valve gear: Overhead
Compression ratio: High; 8.8:1, Low: 8.0:1
Max power: 94 bhp @ 5,500 rpm (from 1964 95 bhp @ 5,400 rpm)
Max torque: 107 lb/ft @ 3,500 rpm (from 1964 110 lb/ft @ 3000 rpm)
Carburation: Twin SU HS4
Transmission
Type: 4 speed, part synchromesh non overdrive
Clutch: Single plate dry, hydraulically operated
Suspension: Front; coil and wishbone, Rear; Live axle with leaf springs
Dampers: Armstrong lever arm front and rear
Steering: Rack and pinion
Brakes: 10.75'' dia front disc. 10'' dia rear drum
Wheels: 4J x 14 pressed steel
Tyres: 5.60 x 14 tubed crossply
Performance
0-60 mph: 12.1 secs
Top speed: 108.1 mph
Fuel consumption: Approx 23 mpg

Specification 1980 MGB
As above except for:
Main bearings: 5
Compression ratio: 9.0:1
Carburation: Twin SU HIF 4
Max Power: 84 bhp @ 5,500 rpm
Max torque: 105 lb/ft @ 2,500 rpm
Transmission: 4 speed all synchromesh with overdrive
Performance:
0-60 mph: 14.0 secs
Top speed: 104 mph
Fuel consumption: approx 25.7 mpg

MGB Roadster Limited Edition

It is worthwhile to look back over the period 1962 to 1980 which is the period that the ever-green MGB was in continuous production at Abingdon. Introduced at the 1962 Motor Show the MGB cost a mere £949 15s 3d and had a top speed of around 108 mph and a 0 to 60mph time of 12.1 secs. With its three main bearing 1798cc engine developing 95 bhp @ 5,400 rpm the MGB was a good performer with plenty of torque throughout the range and was overall a more flexible car than its predecessor, the MGA. The MGB LE announced in October 1980 alongside the GT LE version went on sale at £6,108 with the GT at £6,576. The top peed had changed little in 18 years with a quoted reduction to 105 mph and a 0 to 60 mph time that remained the same. Maximum power quoted to DIN standard was 97 bhp @ 5,500 rpm.

In the intervening years there were numerous modifications to the MGB, some minor, some major. Although the basic body shape remained totally unaltered most of the production changes were cosmetic but some centred on mechanical improvement and as a guide to the evolution of the MGB it would be appropriate to list the main changes and improvements that have taken place over the years. EX 205 as the MGB was codenamed by Abingdon, went into production in May 1962 and had a four speed, three synchromesh non-overdrive gearbox mated to a three main bearing 1798 cc engine. The first change to specification was the option of a Laycock overdrive in January 1963 to be followed by the availability of a factory hardtop in June. Closed circuit crankcase breathing was introduced in February 1965 to be closely followed by a change to a five main bearing engine. An oil cooler now became standard equipment which was available as an option previously. At the same time the dynamo driven rev counter was replaced by an electronic variety. In March 1965 the fuel tank capacity was increased from 10 gallons to 12 together with a change from pull-type door handles to push button, this coincided with the door locks and internal door mechanisms being altered.

In October 1965 the closed coupé version, the MGB GT was announced and this was fitted with a stronger Salisbury type rear axle as opposed to the banjo type. This improvement was not seen on the Roadster until April 1967.

In October of the same year the Mark II version was announced with the following mechanical improvements: dynamo changed for alternator with negative earth electrics, pre-engaged starter to replace the bendix type and a full synchromesh gearbox was fitted. At the same time the transmission tunnel was enlarged to accommodate the now optional Borg Warner automatic transmission. The American market cars now differed to meet more stringent regulations and had emission control equipment, dual circuit brakes and energy absorbing steering columns fitted. The MGC arrived in 1968 and during this year the MGB had changes to the rear axle ratios on both overdrive and non-overdrive cars to be followed in 1969 with a standard closer ratio gearbox. On the export cars Rostyle wheels were fitted as were reclining seats. At the latter end of 1969 the MGB appeared for the first time with a 'British Leyland' badge adorning the front wings. 5 stud Rostyle wheels were standardised with optional wire wheels available. The unpopular recessed front grille with narrow plated surround and vertical black slats was fitted at this time together with a smaller flatter spoked steering wheel. The horn push was now stalk mounted. Leather seats gave way to the reclining vinyl covered variety. From late 1970 the overriders now had black rubber facings and the bonnet and bootlids had telescopic stays fitted. A new Michelotti designed foldaway hood and improved heating and ventilation completed this years improvements.

In October 1971 the Mark III saw yet more changes to the interior with a new centre console and armrest and the radio aperture moving to the console. Fresh air vents now occupied the old radio aperture. Rocker switches replaced toggle switches and a collapsible steering column was introduced now on the UK cars. A year later the front grille is again revised with the MG badge much more prominent set in a chrome surrounded honeycomb plastic mesh. Black wiper arms and blades, door arm rests and a new leather bound steering wheel with slotted spokes, together with a cigar lighter were introduced. The MGB GT V8 was launched in August 1973 and in September 1973 the underbonnet layout of the MGB was commonised with the V8. Radial tyres now became standard and the automatic gearbox option was withdrawn. Servo assisted

brakes were now standard together with hazard warning lights.Then in September 1974 came the most radical of external changes with the introduction of the black impact absorbing polyurethane bumpers front and rear with the front incorporating the grille and indicators. The ride height was raised 1 1/2" to meet US safety legislation. A single 12 volt battery replaced the twin 6 volt batteries. In June 1975 Laycock LH overdrive now became a standard fitment and from August 1976 the suspension was modified with thicker front anti-roll bar and the addition of a rear one. The steering became lower geared and radiator cooling was now by means of a thermostatically controlled electric fan. Overdrive was now selected by gear knob mounted switch and Halogen lights were fitted as standard. The interior was yet again redesigned with striped fabric seats and carpets were fitted throughout instead of rubber matting. The MGB carried sunvisors and the hood now had a zip-out rear window. A new console housed a clock and illuminated switches and an 'H' pattern padded steering wheel. Petrol tank capacity was now reduced to 11 gallons from 12. From late 1977 there was an option of Triumph Stag type wheels with 185/70 tyres and inertia reel seat belts were standard. In January 1978 twin radio speakers were mounted in the door panels. Finally the last 1000 MGBs were produced and completed in October 1980 and designated the Limited Edition. The LEs were fitted with front chin spoilers and the distinctive Stag-type alloy wheels. Wire wheels were an option on the roadster version and the car was finished in bronze metallic paint with gold LE stripes running the length of the car bodywork. The interior was upholstered in orange and brown striped cloth trim and this last of the line MGB carried a price tag of £6,445. A total of 420 Roadsters and 580 GTs were made before the closure of Abingdon and the last of each model now reside with the Rover Group Heritage Trust alongside their famous collection of historic vehicles at the Heritage Centre, Gaydon. Eric Nicholls, a collector of the Limited Edition MGBs and GTs is the owner of the featured car.

The Bronze (Edition of 420).

THE MGB LIMITED EDITION.

MG announce a rare and final edition of the most loved, most famous sports car that has ever been built. The MGB Limited Edition is one thousand cars only, in metallic pewter or bronze, with special distinguishing livery. Two are being acquired by the BL Heritage Collection. The remaining 998 are being offered for sale to members of the public. For availability, contact your BL showroom, or telephone 021-779 2296.

The Silver (Edition of 580).

THE MG CAR COMPANY LIMITED.

CONSCIRE

MGB ROADSTER
LIMITED EDITION

SPECIFICATION

Engine

No of cylinders: 4

Valve operation: overhead operated by tappets, pushrods and rockers.

No of bearings: 5 main.

Bore & Stroke: 80.26mm x 88.9mm

Capacity: 1798cc.

Power output: 97 bhp at 5,500rpm.

Maximum Torque: 105 lb/ft at 2,500 rpm.

Compression ratio: 9.0:1

Carburation: Twin SU HIF4.

Transmission: 4 forward speed, 1 reverse all synchromesh.

Clutch: Single dry plate, hydraulically operated.

Suspension: front; coil and wishbone. rear; live axle with leaf springs.

Dampers: Armstrong lever arm front & rear.

Steering: Rack and pinion.

Brakes: Hydraulic with servo assistance. front; 10.75" dia disc. rear; 10" dia drum.

Acceleration: 0-60 mph; 14 secs. Max. speed; 105 mph.

MGB GT Limited Edition

Very much part of MGB history is the MGB Roadster Limited Edition and its closed coupé counterpart the MGB GT Limited Edition. These cars were built at Abingdon in 1979 and were in fact the last MGs to be built at the famous factory before its closure in October 1980. The MGB was originally launched in 1962 and can be described as the world's most successful sports car with over half a million examples being produced during its 18 year span of continuous production. It was by far the most popular British car to be sold in America since the war and it should be borne in mind that the MGB had two derivatives giving the sports car enthusiast an unrivalled choice of both open topped and closed GT motoring. The big advantage of the GT was that it had most of the attributes of the open top car but could accommodate a family if necessary. The basic shape of the MGB and GT remained virtually the same throughout its production life apart from the post 1975 cars sporting impact resistant black bumpers front and rear. There were some obvious mechanical and cosmetic changes made to the MGB along the way but there is no doubt that the MGB was ahead of its time when introduced in 1962 and had not dated by 1980 when production ceased and it was regarded by many as the best looking sports car of the sixties and seventies.

EX 205, the Abingdon codename for the MGB was conceived as early as 1958 as the replacement for the highly successful MGA and this was before the last of the MGA model range, the MGA 1600 was put into production. There was a design exercise undertaken by the Italian coachbuilders, Frua codenamed EX 214 which had quite stunning lines and a very pleasing appearance apart from a rather aggressive front end. This prototype unfortunately never went into production and all efforts were concentrated on EX 205 which took four years to develop. It was anticipated that the MGB would only have a production life of seven years however the car survived three major corporate reorganisations through from British Motor Corporation that was absorbed into Leyland Motor Corporation which then became Leyland Cars and ultimately BL Cars in 1978. In 1975 the Triumph TR7 made its debut which in the long term was one factor which brought about the demise of the ageing MGB, however the MGB did have a very enthusiastic following in the home market but in 1979 with a very strong Pound Sterling against an ailing American Dollar the export

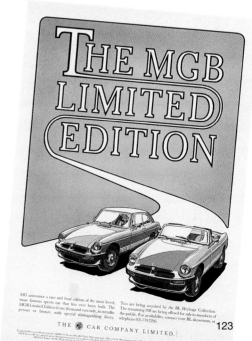

market collapsed. Over 70% of Abingdon production went to the United States and with this very important market in such decline and no suitable replacement model in view, MGB production sadly ceased in 1980 and with it dis-

appeared the famous Abingdon factory that had been the home of MG for 51 years.

When launched the MGB was an all-new car in many respects and was distinguished by its unitary body and chassis structure. It was however not the first British sports car to be built this way, as this type of construction was first utilised on the Austin Healey Sprite, Sunbeam Alpine and MG Magnette as early as 1959. The monocoque construction allowed Abingdon engineers to increase the size of the passenger compartment and reduce the overall length of the car compared to its predecessor the MGA. This was achieved by moving the front limits of the compartment forward 6 inches and increasing the width of the cockpit by one inch, all this was made a lot easier without the hindrance of chassis cross members. As a result there was a lot more leg room and luggage space, all in a car that shared the same 262 cubic feet as the MGA. Although the MGB was technically brilliant and had eye catching features, it was a complicated car to produce and the tooling costs were very high. It required a long production run to recover these costs and as previously mentioned this was projected at seven years, it goes without saying that these costs were recouped over and over again.

The GT version, designated EX 227, a very stylish 3 door hatchback and often referred to as 'the poor man's Aston Martin' did not appear until the Autumn of 1965 and went on sale at £998 which was £143 more than the Roadster. The GT gave considerably more accommodation than the Roadster with an occasional rear seat that would carry preteenage children and fold down to give a very usable load/luggage platform. With the additional weight of 251 lbs, the GT was not such a good performer as the Roadster acceleration wise, however its superior aerodynamics gave it a higher top speed of over 100 mph. The third door/tailgate gave good access to the luggage area and made it overall a more practical sports car. The Italian design studio of Pininfarina were responsible for the GTs very pleasing lines and it was one of the first mass production cars to benefit from the relatively

newly developed computer aided design techniques. Pressed Steel Fisher of Swindon who made up the body shells for final assembly at Abingdon received full sized film drawings direct from Italy which were then very rapidly converted to the production drawings, saving considerably on time and cost. Many of the Roadster components were common to the GT although it carried some that were unique mainly, doors, wings and obviously the roof. The GT carried on in volume production right up until 1980 and the Limited Edition GT featured was ostensibly produced to celebrate 50 years of production at Abingdon but sadly as already described the LE MGs were to mark the end of MG car production at Abingdon.

The 'end of the line' MGBs were fitted with front spoilers and on the Roadster version with the choice of distinctive alloy wheels or wire spoke wheels. (212 cars were fitted with alloy wheels and 208 cars had wire wheels) The Roadster version was finished in bronze metallic with gold LE side stripes running the length of the car bodywork. The inside of the car was upholstered in orange and brown striped cloth trim and it was on sale for £6,445. The GT LE was finished in pewter metallic with silver side stripes and sported a silver grey interior, it carried a price tag of £6,937. A total of 1,000 Limited Edition MGBs were produced, 420 in Roadster form, 580 in GT form with the very last of each model going to the Rover Group Heritage Trust Museum at Gaydon to add to their collection of historic vehicles. The 1980 MGB GT LE featured belongs to Eric Nicholls.

123

MGB GT
LIMITED EDITION

SPECIFICATION

Engine

No of cylinders: 4

Valve operation: overhead operated by tappets, pushrods and rockers.

No of bearings: 5 main.

Bore & Stroke: 80.26mm x 88.9mm

Capacity: 1798cc.

Power output: 97 bhp @ 5,500rpm.

Maximum Torque: 105 lb/ft @ 2,500 rpm.

Compression ratio: 9.0:1

Carburation: Twin SU HIF4,

Transmission: 4 forward speed, 1 reverse all synchromesh.

Clutch: Single dry plate, hydraulically operated.

Suspension: front; coil and wishbone. rear; live axle with leaf springs.

Dampers: Armstrong lever arm front & rear.

Steering: Rack and pinion.

Brakes: Hydraulic with servo assistance. front; 10.75" dia disc. rear; 10" dia drum.

Acceleration: 0-60 mph; 14 secs.

Max. speed: 104 mph.

MGB Roadster
American Limited Edition

The USA specification LE Roadster was one of the last MGs to grace the American highways before production finally ceased at Abingdon in 1980. In view of the fact that none of the modern MG hatchbacks and saloons have found their way across the Atlantic the LE has become something of collectors car. There is no firm indication of the numbers of American specification LEs that were produced, certainly there were several thousand, which is considerably more than their UK counterparts of which 420 roadsters and 580 GTs were made. The American version was produced slightly ahead of the UK LEs in 1979 and was supposed to celebrate 30 years of success in the American sports car market. It was the TC Midget that was really the first MG to be exported to the States in any numbers back in the late forties and helped earn the often quoted phrase; 'MG, the sports car America first loved'.

The American LE was seen by many as a last ditch attempt to revive flagging sales in the USA. This was due in the main to a very low dollar that was pitched against a very high pound sterling which had soared to record levels after a change of British Government in May 1979. This was disastrous news for the British car industry, particularly sports car manufacturers who relied heavily on the American export market, it also hit exports to other countries that purchased imports with dollars. During the summer of 1979 it was claimed that a loss of £900 was made on each MG sold in the States because of huge rebates that were applied to the cars to try and entice prospective purchasers into the showrooms. Even with such incentives the cars were expensive and many remained unsold. Vast numbers did not even make it to the dealers and were unceremoniously crammed into storage lots on the quayside of the docks were they had disembarked the transatlantic freighters.

Another reason for the disappointing sales was the fact that due to ever increasing American safety and emission control regulations, the MGBs performance was less than startling and although there was a 55 mph speed limit in force on all American highways this was virtually all the poor MGB could achieve! The downward slide in cropping the performance of what was then, certainly in the home market version, still an exhilarating car began in 1974. The Federal US regulations stipulated that a 5 mph impact should cause no damage to safety related systems such as brakes, steering, and lighting. The Californian State regulations went a stage further and demanded that there should be no damage at all sustained to the car structure and as a result MG, mindful of the huge importance of the American market to them, decided to comply immediately and were the first British manufacturer to do so. As a result, huge steel armatures were fitted front and rear of the MGB and were covered with black polyurethane moulded bumpers. This did wonders for the resistance to damage in low speed accidents, but nothing for the roadholding or performance. The ride height had to be

increased by 1½ inches to comply with the regulations which affected the centre of gravity, that in turn introduced excessive roll-over-steer on hard cornering. The additional weight of these bumpers of over 70 lbs added insult to injury, penalising the cars performance, which was further restricted by stringent emission control equipment.

The North American specification MGBs carried a small valve cylinder head and a single Zenith Stromberg carburettor instead of the twin SUs together with a very effective air cleaning system. The Californian cars had to comply with even more strict emission controls and had a catalytic converter fitted to the

exhaust manifold to absorb the residual carbon monoxide. This in itself added other problems to the already strangled engine. An air compressor had to be belt driven off the front pulley to inject air into the manifold thus swallowing up even more power from the engine. The end result was a reduction of over 28 bhp from the standard home market car and it is hardly surprising that the car became known in the Abingdon works as "the gutless wonder". The company were obviously not keen to advertise this dramatic drop in power as again it would do little to help sell what had previously been a performance car. No output power figures were quoted in any sales literature, but a Road and Track road test on the LE in 1980 showed a disappointing 67 bhp @ 4,900 rpm, which was little more than that of the mid-fifties ZB Magnette.

Distinguishing features of the American MGB Limited Edition were the silver MGB side stripes, Triumph Stag type alloy road wheels, a special Limited Edition plaque mounted on the glovebox lid, a heavy duty chrome plated boot-mounted luggage rack, a leather rimmed alloy spoked steering wheel, coco floor mats and a front air dam (spoiler). Other features of the export MGBs were the side repeater lamps, red on the rear wing and amber on the front wing, and the rear light clusters which had the positions of the brake and indicator lenses transposed compared to the home market cars. Another feature that was a requirement of the safety regulations, were the triple windscreen wipers which ensured that the largest possible area of the windscreen was cleared by the wipers in adverse weather conditions.

In view of the poor sales climate in 1979/80 many of the American LEs remained unsold for considerable periods, there were some that were never shipped across the Atlantic. Many of these found their way into Europe in standard form but some stayed in the UK and became the subject of V8 or turbo conversions through MG specialist companies who then sold them on the continent. Other cars were purchased by UK enthusiasts who were happy to drive left hand drive cars although an immediate requirement was to remove all the restrictive emission control equipment. One car that is now resident in the UK and re-instated to full North American specification is the concours example featured belonging to enthusiast Eric Nicholls.

127

MGB ROADSTER
AMERICAN LIMITED EDITION

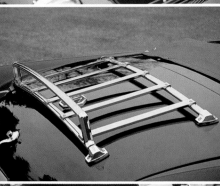

SPECIFICATION

Engine
No of cylinders: 4.
Valve operation: overhead, operated by tappets.
No of bearings: 5 main.
Bore & Stroke: 80.26mm x 88.9mm.
Capacity: 1798 cc.
Power output: 67 bhp at 4,900 rpm.
Max torque: 94 lb/ft at 2,500 rpm.
Compression ratio: 8.0:1.
Carburation: Single Zenith 150CD4T.
Fuel: Unleaded 91 octane.
Transmission: 4 forward speed, 1 reverse all synchromesh.
Clutch: Single dry plate.
Suspension: front; coil and wishbone. rear; live axle with leaf springs.
Dampers: Armstrong hydraulic lever arm.
Steering; Rack and pinion.
Brakes: Hydraulic with servo assistance; front, 10.75" dia disc. Rear; 10" dia drum.
Acceleration: 0-60mph; 13.6 secs.
Maximum speed: 94 mph.
Price new in 1980: $8,900

MGB GT V8

The MGB GT V8 can undoubtedly claim Classic Car status with only 2591 cars produced between December 1972 and September 1976. The car may not even have

materialised at all, had it not been for the enterprise of Ken Costello, who had his own engineering business in Kent. Ken began marketing a V8 conversion of the MGB that sold for £2,400 in 1970. This was a particularly successful conversion, because the 3528cc Rover engine was only a few pounds heavier than the standard cast iron 1798 cc unit. Experiments were carried out at Abingdon as early as 1967 on the fitting of a V8 engine, when both the Daimler 2.5 litre and 4.5 litre units had been shoehorned under MG bonnets, but nothing ever came of them. Costello was able to fit the V8 unit quite neatly under the bonnet with only a small bulge to accommodate the carburation. This conversion gave the car vastly improved acceleration, a top speed in excess of 125 mph and was relatively inexpensive. Because of the extensive publicity that his car received, there is no doubt that British Leyland were prompted to produce their own version. The MGC bodyshell which would have been strong enough for the V8 engine was scrapped in 1969, BL considered that the standard MGB bodyshell was not up to the job and explored the possibilities of producing a GT version. They stopped supply of the all-aluminium Rover V8 to Costello and embarked on a hurried development programme at the Abingdon. Engineers found that the standard MGB gearbox would not cope with the tremendous torque put out by the Rover engine, but were unable to utilise the new 5 speed box developed by Rover, because all that could be produced, were needed for the forthcoming Rover SD1. Ultimately the MGC gearbox was used with modifications.

There were objections from the Triumph division of British Leyland, as executives there did not like the idea of an MGB GT V8 that was potentially faster than their TR6 sports car and Stag tourer, and they were afraid that their sales would suffer dramatically. There was pressure from them to drop the MGB GT anyway, in favour of the new TR7 and it looked likely that the American crash regulations

would exclude open top cars by 1975 which is why the TR7 was produced in hard top form to start with.

It was Lord Stokes, then the Chairman of British Leyland, who gave the go-ahead for the production of the MGB GT V8 as he felt that BL should be able to do a better job than private enterprise. It seems that due to internal politics between MG and Triumph, the MGB GT V8 was only intended as a short term project, to be replaced by the TR8, a V8 version of the TR7. This car could at some later date be produced as an "MG" by the well tried tactic of badge engineering. The MGB GT V8 seemed doomed from the start, because only two months after it's introduction in August 1973, Israel was at war with the Arabs and the West was to experience its worst fuel crisis since 1956. Very soon a 50 mph speed limit was imposed on Britains roads and everyones' attention was turned to fuel economy and away from high performance, large engined cars were definitely out for the time being, although it was a myth that the V8 was uneconomical with the car able to return 25 to 28 mpg. Another factor that was to go against the V8 was the fact that dealers in America were strongly against the idea of selling the car in the United States, because they already were having problems selling the ageing Jaguar E type and the Triumph Stag.

Consequently no left-hand drive versions were produced, other than prototypes, and the car would not even appear on the European market. Seven cars were produced to US specification and were sent over for evaluation, but were eventually returned. One or two of these prototypes have found their way into private owners hands in Europe.

Stiff competition from manufacturers such as Ford who were marketing the Capri well, meant that the V8 was only to sell very slowly in the early stages of its production life. One criticism that was levelled by potential customers was that the car did not look dramatically different from the standard MGB GT, the only real distinguishing features being the wheels which were the strong Dunlop type as used on the Reliant Scimitar. They were very attractive chromed steel rims, riveted to cast

alloy centres, but had less offset than those used by Reliant. 175 x 14 HR tyres were fitted as standard.

Mechanically the car utilised some of the standard MGB GT components, but with the following differences. The gearbox was basically MGC but strengthened and modified to take a larger clutch with higher intermediate gears to withstand the greater torque. For the same reason the overdrive was uprated and made inoperative in third gear, although some of the early cars had overdrive on third and top. A larger diameter propeller shaft was utilised driving through an MGC rear axle but with a lower final drive ratio. This was mounted on uprated rear springs to counter the greater torque reaction. Standard front coil spring suspension was retained at the front with uprated shock absorbers and wishbone mounting rubbers. The braking system was also uprated with a Lockheed servo fitted as standard and larger front discs of greater thickness. Modifications were needed to the cooling system with a larger capacity radiator being fitted further forward in the engine compartment, together with twin electric cooling fans. A remote oil filter assembly was fitted and a high output alternator. Heavy cast iron exhaust manifolds and a specially designed inlet manifold completed the package .

Interior wise, the V8 was very similar to the standard MGB GT, but with the following differences. The steering column was energy absorbing utilising the US specification equipment together with column mounted controls for the wipers and overdrive. This necessitated a larger column shroud, meaning that the speedometer and rev counter had to be reduced in size. Apart from tinted Sundym glass all round as standard, there were no other cosmetic differences. V8 production was nearly always held up by a shortage of engines from Rover and in the four years that the car was in production only 2591 vehicles were produced. In June 1976 British Leyland announced the long awaited Rover SD1 which was inevitably to use the 3.5 litre V8 and 4 weeks later the MGB GT V8 ceased production. It is worth noting that out of the 2591 cars produced between December 1972 and September 1976 (the car was launched to the public in August 1973) 1839 cars were chrome bumper versions and 752 were built with the black impact absorbing bumpers. The concours MGB GT V8 featured is owned by Bill Donaldson.

V8

SPECIFICATION:

Engine: 8 cylinder in 90 degree V formation

Bore/stroke: 88.9 x 71.1mm.

Capacity: 3,528cc

Compression Ratio: 8.25:1

Valve Operation: Single camshaft chain driven from crankshaft operated by pushrods and rockers. Hydraulic tappets.

Carburation: Two constant vacuum SU HIF6 carburettors, horizontally mounted.

Power output: 137 bhp at 5,000 rpm.

Max. Torque: 193lb ft at 2,900 rpm.

Gearbox & Clutch: Four speed all-synchromesh manual gearbox with Laycock overdrive as standard. Borg & Beck 9.5'' dia clutch.

Rear Axle: Salisbury with 3.07:1 ratio as standard.

Suspension: Front; independent by upper and lower wishbones, with coil springs and anti-roll bar. Lever arm hydraulic dampers. Rear; live axle, half-elliptic leaf springs. Lever arm hydraulic dampers.

Wheels and Tyres: Dunlop ventilated cast alloy centre on steel chrome rim, 4 stud fixing, 175 HR14 radial tyres.

Brakes: Lockheed front wheel discs and rear drums. Single hydraulic circuit with servo assistance.

Steering: Cam gear rack and pinion with safety collapsible steering column.

Wheelbase: 7' 7''.

Track: Front 4' 1'', rear 4' 1.25''.

Length: (Chrome bumper) 12' 10.7'', (black bumper) 13' 2.25''.

Width: 5' 0''.

Height: 4' 2''.

Number Built: (Chrome bumper) 1839. (Black bumper) 742. Total production 2591.

Performance: 0-60 mph 7.7 secs. Max speed 125 mph. Standing quarter mile 15.8 secs. MPG approx 26.

Price: New in 1973 £1,925 rising to £3,317 in 1976.

Metro 1300 Saloon

Described as the most anticipated new car in the history of the British Motor Industry, the BL Metro was officially launched to the public on October 8th 1980. It was the long awaited replacement for the ageing Mini and some time prior to the launch became known as the 'Super Mini' project. The codename ADO 88 had been applied to the first prototypes and it was as early as 1975 that the seeds had been sown for the Mini successor. The project was often referred to as the car industry's most publicised 'secret project', more seemed to be known about the car by the press than BL themselves! BLs future depended upon this car more than one could imagine, with £270 million pounds investment, principally in new factories housing the latest in robot technology, the Metro just had to be a winner, it was a do or die situation.

After two years of intensive development that had cost millions in manhours alone, it was decided to scrap the ADO 88 project. This was due in the main to very unfavourable responses in market research and consumer tests. So the Mini replacement was effectively killed off in favour of a slightly larger car. The decision was also taken at the same time to keep the Mini in production alongside this new project which was to be codenamed LC8. The codes had now changed from the old ADO (Austin Drawing Office) to LC (Leyland Cars) and at the start of 1978 a full sized mock-up of the LC8 was set up in a Paris Hotel and put before an invited audience for appraisal. This exercise was repeated in other cities in Europe and the project was deemed highly suitable as a 'Euro Car' standing up well against competition from Volkswagen Fiat and Renault. Thus was born the Metro shape that we know today.

There is little doubt that very early on in the development of the Metro, there were plans for up-market and high performance versions. These eventually took the form of the luxuriously appointed Vanden Plas and of course the high performance MG 1300. There were precedents for marketing the Metro with an MG badge on it in the form of the MG 1100 and 1300 saloons of the sixties. These performance versions of the standard Austin and Morris cars sold very well indeed and showed just how popular and commercially attractive

the MG marque was. Many thought that there may have been an MG version of the Mini in view of the success of the 1100s and 1300s and it is not widely known that had the Cooper and Cooper 'S' variants of the Mini not sold so well an MG version was very much on the cards and had in fact been mocked up in the design studios. Due to the strong following of the Cooper badged Minis it would perhaps have seemed logical to have extended the name to the performance version of the Metro, but this would have involved BL in royalties and trade mark problems and anyway they had two redundant 'sporting' marques in the name of Triumph and MG. Just a few weeks before the public launch of the Metro the decision was taken to call the performance version an MG.

In April and May 1982, BL announced the

Vanden Plas and MG versions respectively and immediately there was outcry from the diehard MG traditionalists that the car was not worthy of the MG badge. The very thought of this 'badge engineering' was greeted by some of the MG fraternity with utter dismay until it was pointed out that this type of exercise was by no means unique in MG history. After the dust had settled and particularly when the MG Metro had received endorsements from the MG Owners' Club and MG Car Club, the car immediately settled into its own niche in the marketplace. BL saw that support from the Clubs was essential and made the unprecedented move of inviting the Clubs to become involved in suggestions on finer detail at the pre-production stage. Both Roche Bentley from the MG Owners' Club and Bill Wallis, then chairman of the MG Car Club attended Longbridge some months before the official launch and were shown the proposed car in the styling studios. They were asked their opinions and as a result some visual changes were made, clearly to give the car more MG emphasis and sporting appeal. Things like octagonal instrument cowls were discussed, such as those that had adorned the old MG saloons, but they were dismissed as just not looking right in a modern day car.

The instructions that the engineers and

designers were given stipulated that the MG Metro had to have comparable performance to the Mini Cooper'S' of the sixties with excellent roadholding and a high level of trim and finish. Although the standard body shell was employed, when compared to the standard Metro the MG version was quite strikingly different. In standard form the Metro 1275 cc 'A' plus series engine developed 60 bhp but the MG sported a higher profile camshaft, larger valves and a twin downpipe exhaust manifold. Carburation was by means of a single SU as opposed to the Cooper 'S' twin SUs. Compression ratio was raised to 10.5:1 with the end result of a meaningful 72 bhp @ 6000 rpm. Brakes, steering and suspension remained virtually standard whilst the pressed steel wheels were replaced with attractive cast alloy wheels bearing low profile tyres. In wind tunnel tests a brand new type of rear spoiler was developed and ultimately fitted, reducing the drag coefficient from the standard 0.41 to 0.39. The transmission was unchanged although the low profile tyres did give overall lower gearing.

The main distinguishing features of the MG 1300 were the numerous MG Octagons on wheel centres, side stripes, front grille, rear tailgate and internally on the front parcel shelf mat, heel mat and finally in the centre of the steering wheel boss. Everything was somewhat overzealously colour keyed red, nonetheless with red seat belts, red trim piping and red stitching to the very comfortable and supportive rally seats, the MG version stood out from the rest of the pack! To follow the sporting feel through a small 14" leather covered dished steering wheel was fitted behind which lay the distinctive instrument console that was unique to the MG. There were no complaints from any quarter concerning the performance or handling of the MG 1300 with 101 mph attainable and a 0-60 mph time of 10.9 seconds the car sold well from the outset. At the time of the launch, the MG Metro was described as the fastest MG saloon ever produced, this has since been topped by MG Metro Turbo, MG Montego Turbo and finally the MG Maestro Turbo which was claimed to have a top speed of 135mph! The MG Metro Turbo was already in the planning before the launch of the standard car and was ready for sale to the public in October 1982. The featured car is a 1983 model belonging to Cathy Barton.

SPECIFICATION
Engine Number of cylinders: 4 in line
Bore & Stroke: 70.61mm x 81.28mm
Capacity: 1275 cc
Compression ratio: 10.5:1
Valve operation: Pushrod overhead valve
Carburation: Single horizontal SU
Power Output: 72 bhp @ 6000 rpm
Transmission Gearbox: 4 speed all synchromesh
Clutch: Single dry plate
Suspension: Independent Hydrogas all-round
Wheels: Bolt-on cast alloy
Brakes: Servo assisted disc at front, drum at rear

Metro Turbo Saloon

In the spring of 1982 BL cars announced up-market derivatives of the Metro. The base model Metro was originally launched in 1980 and billed as one of the most publicised 'secret' projects of the British Motor Industry. The up-market versions were the sporty MG and the luxurious Vanden Plas, however there was an outcry from the diehard MG traditionalists that the Metro was not worthy of an MG badge. There is no doubt that from very early on in the development of BLs super mini that there were plans to produce high performance models of the car. There were precedents for marketing such a car particularly with an MG badge on it, although there had never been an MG Mini. It is not widely known but had the Austin and Morris badged Mini Coopers and Cooper S's not sold as well as they did, an MG version was very much on the cards. The precedents for marketing an MG version of the Metro were in the form of the MG 1100 and 1300 saloons of the 1960's. These up-market versions of the standard Austin and Morris cars sold particularly well and illustrated just how popular and commercially attractive the MG marque was.

In view of the previous success of the Cooper badged Minis it would have seemed logical to continue with the name on the performance Metro, however this would probably have meant that BL would have had to pay royalties and anyway they had some redundant sporting marques on their books, namely Triumph and MG . It was not until a few weeks before the public launch of the standard Metro in October 1980 that the decision was taken to call the sporting version an MG. The initial reaction by the MG fraternity was one of dismay as previously described. The very thought of this badge engineering was taken almost as sacrilege until it was pointed out that this type of exercise was by no means unique in MG history.

What was unprecedented in MG history was the fact that the MG Clubs were invited to become involved in suggestions on finer detail at the pre-production stage of the car. Both Roche Bentley from the MGOC and Bill Wallis of the MGCC were invited to Longbridge some months before the official launch and were shown the proposed car in the styling studios. They were asked for their opinions and as a result some visual changes were made to the car mainly to give the car more MG emphasis. A suggestion that octagonal instrument could be used, similar to those employed on the earlier MG saloons was turned down on the grounds that they just did not look right. Side stripes and colour keyed seat belts were other features that received total support.

The brief in preparing the MG was to give the car equal performance of the Cooper S's of the sixties, with comparable roadholding but a higher level of trim and finish. The basic body shell was identical to the standard car, however when compared with the standard Metro the MG was quite strikingly different. In standard form the 1275 cc transversely mounted engine produced 60 bhp but the MG version was to have a higher profile camshaft, bigger valves and a twin downpipe exhaust manifold. The carburation was to be by a single SU as opposed to the Cooper S's twin SUs. Compression ratio was higher though at 10.5:1 as opposed to 9.71:1. This gave an increase in bhp to 72 @ 6000 rpm. The brakes, steering and suspension of the standard Metro were retained except that the normal pressed steel wheels were replaced with attractive cast alloy ones bearing low profile tyres. The gearbox also did not change however the low profile tyres gave slightly lower overall gearing. In wind tunnel tests it was decided to employ an entirely new type of rear spoiler fitted to the hatchback tailgate. This was moulded in plastic and an inverted 'U' shape that almost shrouded the rear screen. There were dramatic improvements in the drag co-efficient from the standard 0.41 to 0.39 on the MG version. This represented at the end of the day an increase of approximately 1.5 miles per gallon at high speed cruising.

Other distinguishing features were obviously numerous MG octagons on wheel centres, side stripes, front grille, rear tailgate stripes and internally on the steering wheel centre boss, parcel tray and embossed into the carpet heel panel. The previously mentioned red seat belts keyed in well with the red piping on the very comfortable and supportive rally type front seats. To add to the drivers comfort a small 14" dished leather covered steering wheel was fitted and behind this there was a distinctive instrument console that was unique to the MG. This carried a 7000 rpm rev

counter, speedometer and warning lights.

At the time of the launch, the MG Metro was billed as the fastest MG saloon ever produced, this has since been claimed of the Metro Turbo and subsequently the MG Montego Turbo with speeds of over 130 mph attainable. The claimed top speed was just over the magic ton at 101 mph, an acceleration time of 0-60 mph was 10.9 secs and quite respectable for a 1275 cc saloon. There were no complaints from any quarter about the performance of the MG Metro, however just five months after its introduction, it was followed by a turbocharged version. This was not just a simple job of bolting on a turbo, there were extensive modifications made to the engine.

Starting with the cylinder head, this was derived from the standard 1.3 unit rather than the MG unit, it had modified water jackets round the valve seats to aid cooling, stronger double valve springs to allow higher engine revs and they were sodium filled to avoid valve seat shrinkage. The crankshaft was nitrided for extra strength and the main bearings were modified to give an increased bearing surface area. Stronger, solid skirt pistons were machined to give a lower compression ratio of 9.4:1. An increased capacity oil pump was fitted that also lubricated the turbocharger bearings. The Garrett Air Research T3 turbocharger hidden between the engine and bulkhead boosted power output to 93 bhp @ 6130 rpm and torque to 851 lbs/ft @ 2650 rpm with its rotors spinning at speeds up to 120,000 rpm. The unit 'blew' through an SU HIF 44 single carburettor and exhausted into a large bore system with straight through silencers.

A highly sophisticated electronic wastegate system ensured that the turbo delivered its boost pressure gradually to avoid the abrupt transition from normally aspirated to virtually full boost from which many turbocharged installations normally suffered. The wastegate was a blow off valve which regulated the maximum boost pressure and was a fail safe measure designed to protect engine components. A recirculating fuel system was incorporated, fed by a high pressure pump and this required a modified petrol tank. Other essential changes included a larger capacity radiator and oil cooler. Suspension and braking was uprated to cope with the 112 mph performance. Ventilated front discs were developed directly from competition Metros to give better heat dissipation. Four piston brake callipers assisted in reducing brake fade. Uprated anti roll bars were fitted together with 10% uprated Hydragas units and dampers.

Internally the Metro Turbo had one or two refinements over the standard Metro, with a side window demisting system, opening rear quarter lights, remote control drivers door mirror, stereo radio/cassette, laminated windscreen and of course not neeeded on the standard car, a LED turbo boost gauge. The distinctive colour keyed sporting red theme was continued in the Metro Turbo throughout the cockpit. Externally the Turbo was identified by a deep moulded black front spoiler that incorporated brake cooling ducts and flared wheel arch extensions. A rear spoiler from the standard MG Metro adorned the rear window and distinctive Turbo side stripes completed the body detail. The finishing touch to the Turbo's appearance was set by 13 inch alloy wheels sporting 165/60 x 13 low profile tyres and extra ventilation louvres at the rear of the bonnet allowed heat dissipation .

METRO Turbo

Specification

Engine

Number of cylinders: 4

Capacity: 1275 cc

Bore & Stroke: 70.61mm x 81.28mm

Compression Ratio: 9.4:1

Valve gear: Pushrod overhead valve

Carburation: Single SU HIF44

Turbocharger: Garrett Air Research T3

Max Boost Pressure: 7.5 psi

Max Power: 93 bhp @ 6130 rpm

Max Torque: 85lb/ft @ 2650 rpm

Transmission

Type: 4 speed all synchromesh

Clutch: Single dry plate

Suspension

Front: Independent bottom link braced by anti roll bar. Top link operating Hydragas spring. Telescopic dampers.

Rear: Independent trailing arms, anti roll bar, coil spring pre loaded on Hydragas unit.

Wheels: Vented cast alloy 13″ diameter, 5.5 J rims

Tyres: Steel braced radial low profile 165/60 VR13.

Brakes: Front – 4 piston caliper ventilated disc. Rear – 7″ drum.

Performance

0-60 mph: 9.9 secs

Max speed: 112 mph

Fuel consumption: 50.3 mpg @ 56 mph (urban)

Metro 6R4

Since its announcement as a concept car in February 1984, the MG Metro 6R4 underwent continuous development both as a rally car and for production to meet the FISA requirements for 200 identical cars to be manufactured. The car challenged Europe's top teams in the World Rally Championships culminating in an historical victory on the Circuit of Ireland Rally on April 1st 1986. It was historical in the sense that David Llewellin was the first driver to take a four wheel drive car to victory on this particular International rally. Leading virtually from the start, the 6R4 won by a margin of some 9 minutes, stealing the limelight from the conventional rear wheel drive Opels that had dominated the circuit for at least seven years. The 6R4 gained several notable firsts at national level with a creditable third position in the Lombard RAC Rally, in the same year.

With the arrival of the MG Metro in early 1982, it was the aim of Austin Rover to repeat the supremacy of the Abingdon prepared Mini Coopers in International rallies and circuit racing during the sixties. This was achieved in part with MG Metros and MG Metro turbos competing in British Saloon Car championships with some success and the MG Metro Challenge provided exciting one make racing, reminiscent of the Mini Cooper era. More excitement was generated over the announcement of the MG Metro 6R4 in February 1984, some 20 years after the Mini Cooper 'S' won the Monte Carlo Rally. The 6R4 was primarily a development project but made a sensational debut into its first rally, recording the fastest times over the first eight stages. The car could not however enter rallies of International status because of the homologation regulations which required 200 identical examples to be built. The homologation requirements were finally met and the 'Clubman' version as it was called was offered for sale to the rallying fraternity at an off-the-shelf price of nearly £35,000, whilst the full International Rally specification car set you back a cool £47,000 and that was excluding VAT!

Because of the two different specifications, there were two versions of the 90 degree V6 engine with the 'International' engine producing a possible hefty 410 bhp and the 'Clubman' a modest 250 bhp! Modifications were available to transform the Clubman engine to International specification through Austin Rover Motorsport. The engines were built alongside the Rover production engines at Austin Rover's Coventry engine plant and the choice of a normally aspirated design instead of turbocharging had considerable benefits. The immense torque available ensured an instant throttle response throughout the whole rev range. Figures quoted were 270 lb ft @ 6500 rpm for the International and 225 lb ft @ 4500 rpm for the Clubman. This was in stark contrast to the characteristics of turbocharged engines which generally had inherent throttle lag and poor low speed torque together with huge underbonnet heat dissipation problems which were considerably reduced with normally aspirated engines. The engine was coded V64V (6 cylinders in vee formation with 4 valves per cylinder) and it was the first engine ever designed specifically for International rallying, instead of being derived from a standard production car unit. The 3 litre engine was of oversquare design in 90 degree V6 configuration with a symmetrical crankshaft and uneven firing. The block and heads were of cast aluminium incorporating design features in their

structure that made them light but rigid. The block had dry liners of iron alloy. The valves (4 per cylinder) were directly operated by twin overhead, belt driven camshafts. At the bottom end of the engine, the cast aluminium dry sump contained the engine oil as well as the short cross shaft between the rear differential and the left hand drive shaft coupling together with the separate lubrication system for the shaft. The rear differential casing bolted to both the block and the sump making a very rigid unit.

Because the engine was mounted 'in reverse' the water pump migrated to the same end as the twin plate AP clutch. The specially designed pump, like so many of the ancillaries was belt driven. The alternator, capable of

delivering over a kilowatt of steady power, was mounted at the rear of the engine in the vee of the block and the lightweight starter motor had an output two and a half times that of the conventional one. There was a digitised fuel and ignition control system devised by Lucas Micos with two different sets of fuel injection hardware. On the 'Clubman' 6R4 there was a single butterfly controlling the air intake but even with this and the Lucas processor, 250 bhp was easily attainable. The other system on the 'International' specification car was a full six butterfly, six venturi induction manifold which gave between 380 bhp and 410 bhp dependent on the requirements of the particular rallies. The whole engine ready to install in the 6R4 weighed in at 140 kilogrammes and apart from the oil cooler and radiator there were no other additional ancillaries.

Worthy of mention is the original prototype engine that was fitted to the 6R4. This was a pushrod V62V engine which achieved far more than was ever expected of it. The V62V was produced very quickly because Austin Rover needed an engine of the right size and weight to power the prototypes. The first engines were made literally by slicing two cylinders out of the well known Rover V8 engine and welding the pieces back together again before final machining and assembly. A special crankshaft had to be designed, but pistons, valves, rocker gear, pushrods, connecting rods and all other external components were from the Rover unit. Induction was by a pair of downdraught, three barrel Webers for simplicity. In this form the engine produced approximately 235 bhp. These engines powered the MG Metro 6R4s throughout 1983 and 1984, first in

private testing and finally on actual events for which they were never intended.

The MG Metro 6R4 was built at Austin Rover's Longbridge car plant and it utilised the latest laser technology coupled with traditional craftsmanship. The differences between the standard Metro and the 6R4 were many with the most obvious in the bodywork. The car was some 70mm wider with consequent increases in front and rear track spanning 1510mm at the front and 1550mm at the rear. Wheelbase was lengthened by 90mm to 2391 mm with most of the increase at the rear of the vehicle. The road wheels were also increased in diameter from 340mm to 390mm which gave greater advantage on loose surfaces and ice and snow when shod with 16" tyres. Another constraint was the fact that most of the advanced development in the construction and compounds of tyres was only available with the larger tyre sizes. Consequently the Metro was persuaded to grow a little to accept them. The wheel arches were enlarged to accommodate the bigger wheel and tyres with the 12" ventilated discs taking advantage of the extra space inside the wheel. Major external changes were the incorporation of a high rear wing and low front wing to aid stability and extensive modifications to the bonnet and front and rear wheel arches took full opportunity of increasing the vertical wheel movement.

The 6R4's suspension was fully adjustable for camber, ride height and castor angle and incorporated Bilstein gas-filled struts which were clamped at their lower end into cast alloy hub carriers. The road wheels were designed by a British company, Dymag who had earned a good reputation in the Formula One field. The purpose designed transmission centred on a five speed gearbox feeding its power to an epicyclic centre differential through a pair of step-off gears. An AP twin-plate clutch provided the link between engine and gearbox and a conventional prop shaft fed the power forward to the front differential while a shaft ran past the engine sump to the rear differential mounted on the side of the engine. This shaft was splined to facilitate rapid differential changes should it have proved necessary. There was a short cross shaft taking power to the left wheel through the engine sump. FF Developments viscous couplings were used in the centre of the 6R4's four wheel drive system and were used on both front and rear differentials.

There was little to differentiate externally between the Clubman and International 6R4's with the only detectable difference being the inclusion of an underbody aerodynamic diffuser on the International car. What was less obvious was the fact that Kevlar was used to construct the wheel arches on the International version giving greater strength with weight saving, whereas on the Clubman car they are made from fibreglass. A test carried out by 'Autocar' magazine showed staggering performance figures for the Computervision 6R4 with a 0-60 mph time of 3.2 seconds, whilst the Clubman version was not far behind with a figure of 4.5 seconds. 'Autocar' stated that it was the fastest accelerating, wheel driven car that they had ever tested. The MG Metro 6R4 put the MG name once more in the forefront of International Motorsport, albeit only briefly as these 'supercars' were soon to be banned by FISA as they were deemed to quick for their own good!

Metro 6R4

Specification

Engine: Mid-engined, all aluminium alloy, 6 cylinder in 90 degree V formation. Dry iron alloy liners. 4 main bearings. Water cooled by electric fan.

Bore and Stroke: 92mm x 75mm

Capacity: 2991cc

Valve Gear: 2 overhead cams per bank. 4 valves per cylinder.

Compression ratio: 12:1

Ignition: Lucas Micos electronic.

Fuel Injection: Lucas Micos six point electronic

Transmission: 5 speed dog engaged manual gearbox with permanent four wheel drive. Borg & Beck twin plate diaphragm clutch 7¼" dia. Viscous centre coupling. Prop shaft drive to front differential, quill shaft drive to rear. Fully articulating drive shafts.

Suspension: Front; Independent, coil spring, strut and bottom wishbone. Bilstein telescopic gas filled dampers, anti-roll bar. Ride height, camber, toe-in and anti-roll are all adjustable.
Rear: Independent, coil spring, strut bottom wishbone and trail link. Bilstein gas filled telescopic dampers, anti-roll bar. Ride height, camber, toe-in and anti-roll are all adjustable.

Steering: Rack and pinion, 2.5 turns lock to lock.

Brakes: Dual circuit, with adjustable ratio split front to rear.
Front: 12″ dia ventilated discs.
Rear: 12″ dia ventilated dics. Four piston calipers all round. Handbrake: hydraulic lever acting on rear discs.

Wheels: Dymag die-cast magnesium alloy with various Michelin tyres dependent on conditions.

Body: Three door bodyshell with glass reinforced plastic wheel arches and sills. Front and rear aerofoils. Fabricated front and rear chassis frames. Two main longitudinal chassis members. Integral full roll cage. Two seats with full rally harness. Fully instrumented dashboard (conventional Metro dash on homologation car)

Wheelbase: 2391mm

Track: Front: 1510mm
Rear: 1550mm

Performance: International spec: 0-60 mph 3.2 seconds. 0-110 mph 10.00 secs.
Clubman spec: 0-60 mph 4.5 seconds. 0-100 mph 12.8 secs.

Maestro 1600 Saloon

In March 1983 the long awaited five-door hatchback range of cars from British Leyland, codenamed LM10 arrived on the scene. Originally designated ADO99 and intended as a direct replacement for the Austin Allegro, the project merged with LM11 (Montego Saloon) and became LM10. Development costs were quite astronomical and they were to be the first generation of cars from BL born of the CAD CAM age and it demonstrated their commitment to this exciting new technology. (CAD standing for Computer Aided Design and CAM standing for Computer Aided Manufacture). Michael Edwardes, during his chairmanship of BL had to make many economies in order to secure the funds for such ambitious projects, not least of which was the demise of Abingdon just 3 years earlier. LM 10 was intended to revitalise the flagging corporate image of BL, now renamed Austin Rover Group and designed to take the company into the late 1980s in a stronger market position. LM10 became the Maestro in March 1983 and the MG variant to be known as the MG Maestro 1600 was amongst the seven strong model launch. This was to be a high performance derivative offering over 110mph from a 102bhp R series engine. Designers were given a brief that it should offer very generous interior dimensions within a compact overall size, exploiting the packaging advantages of front wheel drive to the full. The overall exterior surface of the car was defined by computer in the design stages and the same computer data was fed to the presses to control the manufacture of the body panels. The Maestro was built at a new high technology plant at Cowley on the outskirts of Oxford where the vast majority of the assembly of the car was carried out by computer controlled robot machines.

A bonus of the computer aided design was that simulated crash tests could be carried out to predict deforming of panels before full crash testing at MIRA. Optimum positioning of seat belt mountings and thicknesses of metal panels were also determined by computer, even the headlamp lenses were designed by computer to provide optimum efficiency coupled with the low bonnet line. These new type of lenses were called Homofocal and in terms of innovative technology, the Maestro was the first British car to feature these. The basic Maestro emerged as a well thought out but slightly uninteresting car, but had the potential as a good "bread and butter" earner. The MG as usual was to be the top of the range high performance derivative and was designed to corner another percentage point of the lucrative medium car market. The MG and Vanden Plas versions carried innovative full electronic instrumentation and a voice synthesis warning system, with the latter causing great consternation amongst the motoring press. The voice unit carried a 32 word vocabulary with messages such as "brake on", "fasten seat belts", "low fuel" and "low oil pressure". Autocar stated that the "Electronic fascia takes a little get-

ting used to" and "Mercifully, to anyone allergic to unsolicited instructions, there is a restrict button!". Motor's view was that if the system insisted on telling you that you needed to fasten your seatbelt when you had already done so, it was a certain way of ensuring that the voice control switch remained in the "off" position. There was also for the first time on a

British car, an advanced solid state electronic instrumentation system that was controlled by two microprocessors. Other than the trip meter there were no other moving parts and instead of the conventional speedometer cable there was an electronic sensor in the gearbox that sent speed signals to the computer which in turn activated vacuum fluorescent displays for engine revs, road speed, temperature and fuel tank level. A novel idea for those using their cars on the continent was the ability at the flick of a switch to change the speedometer reading from miles to kilometres per hour. Considering that the electronic gadgetry added nearly £200 to the selling price of the car it was a pity that the early dashboards were inaccurate and prone to premature failure.

Only two engines were planned for the seven model range, one was the tried and tested evergreen A series 1275cc unit and the other was a brand new 1598 cc R series engine that had its parentage in the Maxi single overhead camshaft E series engine. The MG was to be powered by a special version of the 1600 cc unit and the desire was to have a high performance engine that was both smooth and tractable as well as exciting. Two twin choke downdraught 40 DCNF carburettors coupled to a low loss 8 port inlet manifold gave the extra power, whilst standard camshaft timing was retained for greater low speed flexibility, however the ports were enlarged from the standard engine. This

increased the power output from a standard 81 bhp to 103 bhp @ 6000rpm. An end mounted close ratio 5 speed Volkswagen gearbox transferred the power to the road wheels which were a radial multi-bar pattern cast alloy type, fitted with Pirelli P8 low profile tyres. Suspension was the same as the standard models apart from a thicker anti-roll bar with the front utilising MacPherson struts and coil springs and at the rear an interconnected torsion bar trailing arm system was adopted. On introduction the MG 1600 was offered at £6245 which was competitively priced alongside the Ford XR3i, Golf GTi and Vauxhall Astra GTE all of which had better acceleration and a higher top speed. The R series engine version of the 1600 Maestro was fairly short lived although 12,427 cars were produced at Cowley before it was replaced in July 1984 with the S Series engine model that had been previously introduced on the new Montego codenamed LM11. Priced at £6,775 the only changes to the 1600 were in the engine department and consisted of a lighter and thinner walled cylinder block, a better balanced crankshaft, a toothed drive for the camshaft, improved distributor drive, new oil pump and water pump. The alloy cylinder head was also redesigned. This premature change of the Maestro power unit simply confirmed suspicions that the car had lacked proper development and hastily put together. This version too was very soon discontinued when only 2,762 cars in total had been produced, before being replaced by the MG Maestro EFi which was announced in October 1984. The immaculate 1984 MG Maestro 1600 featured, bearing an S series engine, is owned by Mark Durocher-Weston.

Maestro 1600

SPECIFICATION

Engine No of cylinders: 4
Capacity: 1598cc
Bore & Stoke: 76.2mm x 87.6mm
Valve gear: Single overhead camshaft
Carburation: Two twin-choke 40 DCNF
Weber carburettors
Power output: 103 bhp @ 6,000 rpm
Top speed: 111 mph
Performance: 0-60 mph in 9.6 secs
Clutch: Single dry plate
Suspension: Independent front, McPherson
strut, semi-independent rear telescopic
with coil springs
Wheels : Cast alloy 14" x 5.5J with 175/65
x 14 tyres
Brakes: Servo assisted, dual line hydraulic,
Front; disc, rear; self adjusting drums
Number built: July to October 1984: 2,762

Maestro 2·0i Saloon

LM 10 as it was codenamed was the first of a new generation of cars that was designed to revitalise the corporate image of the Austin Rover Group and to take the company into the late 1980s in a stronger market position. Hence LM10 became the Maestro in March 1983 and amongst the seven strong model launch there was an MG variant known as the Maestro 1600. This was to be a high performance derivative offering over 110mph from a 102bhp R series engine. The original design brief for the Maestro was that it should offer exceptionally generous interior dimensions within a compact overall size, exploiting the packaging advantages of front wheel drive to the full. It was the first of BL's cars to be born of the CAD CAM age and demonstrated their commitment to this exciting new technology. (CAD standing for Computer Aided Design and CAM standing for Computer Aided Manufacture). The total exterior surface of the car was defined by computer in the design stages and the same computer data was utilised to control the manufacture of the body panels. The Maestro was built at a new high technology plant at Cowley on the outskirts of Oxford where the vast majority of the assembly of the car was carried out by computer controlled robot machines.

Additional applications of the computer aided design included simulated crash tests to predict deforming of panels before full crash testing. Optimum positioning of seat belt mountings and thicknesses of metal panels were also determined by computer, even the headlamp lenses were designed by computer to provide optimum efficiency coupled with the low bonnet line. These new type of lenses were called Homofocal and in terms of innovative technology, the Maestro was the first British car to feature these, along with impact resistant colour-matched integrated polyester bumpers and on the top models (MG included) full electronic instrumentation and a voice synthesis warning system. There were to be only two engines available for the seven model range, one was the tried and tested evergreen A series 1275 cc unit and the other was a brand new 1598cc R series engine that was loosely based on the Maxi single overhead camshaft E series engine. A special version of the 1600 cc unit was to power the MG version and the brief was to have a high performance engine that was both smooth and tractable as well as exciting. The unit was fitted with two twin choke downdraught 40 DCNF carburettors coupled to a low loss inlet manifold for extra power. Standard camshaft timing was retained for greater low speed flexibility, however the ports were enlarged. This increased the power output from a standard 81 bhp to 102 bhp @ 6000rpm . An end mounted close ratio 5 speed Volkswagen gearbox transferred the power to

the road wheels which were cast alloy shod with Pirelli P8 low profile tyres.

Suspension was the same as the standard models apart from a thicker anti-roll bar with the front utilising MacPherson struts and coil springs and at the rear an interconnected torsion bar trailing arm system was adopted. On the MG 1600 and Vanden Plas versions only, there was for the first time on a British car, an advanced solid state electronic instrumentation system fitted that was controlled by two microprocessors. Other than the trip meter there were no other moving parts. Instead of the conventional speedometer cable there was an electronic sensor in the gearbox that sent speed signals to the computer which in turn activated vacuum fluorescent displays for engine revs, road speed, temperature and fuel

tank level. A novel idea for those using their cars on the continent was the ability at the flick of a switch to change the speedometer reading from miles to kilometres per hour. Also novel was the provision of a voice synthesis unit that carried a 32 word vocabulary. This supplemented the electronic instruments and broad-

cast such messages as 'fasten seatbelts', 'low fuel', 'handbrake on', and 'low oil pressure'. The price of the 1600 Maestro on introduction was £6245 and was competitively priced alongside the Ford XR3i, Golf GTi and Vauxhall Astra GTE all of which had better acceleration and a higher top speed. The car was unfortunately not received well by the motoring press as it was fairly evident that the car was underdeveloped and rushed to meet the launch date. The main problems centred around the carburation that did not seem suited to the crossflow engine. Hot starting was particularly a problem and many writers felt that the car 'ran out of steam above 6000rpm'. The Weber version of the 1600 Maestro was fairly short lived and was replaced with the S Series engine that had been introduced on LM11, the Montego. This unit differed from the earlier R series engine in that it had a lighter and thinner walled cylinder block, a better balanced crankshaft, a toothed drive for the camshaft, improved distributor drive, oil pump and water pump. The cylinder head was also redesigned. This premature change of the Maestro power unit simply confirmed suspicions that the car had been hastily put together and this version too was very soon discontinued when less than 3000 cars in total had been produced.

The MG Maestro EFi was announced in October 1984 and was a far better car than its 1600 predecessor. This car ultimately became known as the MG 2.0i and was a vast improvement particularly as it employed a fuel injected two litre 0 series engine that produced 115bhp. This power unit had the benefit of fully programmed ignition with knock sensing and the Lucas 'L' type multi point fuel injection system. A new close ratio 5 speed gearbox of Honda design transferred the power. Performance was quite respectable with a 0-60 mph time of 8.5 secs. To cater for the increased performance the front brakes were uprated and fitted with ventilated discs and tyres were uprated from SR to HR specification. Suspension was modified with a rear anti-roll bar fitted as standard. Cosmetic changes were kept to a minimum, however the interior benefitted from a new velour trim and a new leather trimmed three spoked steering wheel. Central door locking and tinted glass became a standard fitment. The exterior was distinguished from the MG 1600 version by a colour keyed front grille, colour keyed door mirrors and door handles and MG motifs on the road wheel centres. Power steering could be ordered as an optional extra. The instrumentation reverted back to standard analogue dials although the electronic dashboard could be ordered as an option. Later versions of the 2.0i carried cross spoked alloy wheels with an option of a manual tilt and slide glass sunroof. The featured car is owned by Dave Ransome.

MAESTRO 2.0i

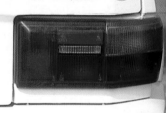

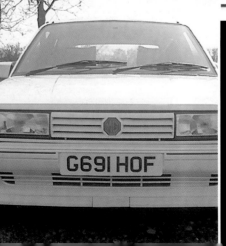

SPECIFICATION
Engine: 'O' series
No of cylinders: 4
Capacity: 1944 cc
Bore & Stroke: 84.5 mm x 89.0 mm
Valve gear: Overhead Camshaft
Fuel system: Lucas Electronic L type
multi-point injection
Power Output: 115 bhp @ 5,500 rpm
Performance: 0-60 mph; 8.5 secs
Clutch: Dry plate
Gearbox: 5 speed all-synchromesh
Suspension: Independent front,
semi-independent rear with coil springs
Wheels: Alloy, bolt-on
Brakes: Ventilated disc front, drums at rear

Montego 2.0i Saloon

Just a year after the successful launch of the Maestro (LM10) its bigger brother the Montego (LM11) was introduced by Austin Rover in April 1984 at a press launch staged in the South of France. The Montego used the existing floorpan of the Maestro but was made wider by 2" in the wheelbase which provided more legroom for the rear seat passengers. About 60% of the panels were the same as the Maestro, but the Montego was strictly a four door saloon and measuring nearly 16" longer than the Maestro was overall a larger car. An extensive boot area offered a generous 18.4 cu ft of space and the rear seat folded down to accommodate long or bulky items such as skis. Steering, brakes and suspension were copied straight from the Maestro, except that the brake discs were ventilated. The 'O' series engine which was originally intended as a new unit for the ageing B series engine that powered the MGB, but only this engine only appeared in a few prototype models. This 2 litre engine destined for the MG Montego Efi had a new alloy cylinder head in which the inlet ports were paired together rather than alternated with the exhaust ports. The drive was through an all new Honda 5 speed gearbox to the front wheels replacing the Volkswagen unit used on the

Maestro stablemate. An electronic ignition system, together with Lucas L type electronic fuel injection returned 115 bhp @ 5500 rpm as opposed to 102 bhp on the normally aspirated engine, with top speed matching the bhp at 115 mph. A 0-60 mph time of 8.9 seconds was more than adequate to show "a clean pair of heels" to much of the competition. An innovation on the MG Maestro was the introduction of computer Liquid Crystal Display instrumentation, this was naturally extended to the new MG Montego Efi, having been further developed, but many customers found it to be rather gimmicky and irritating. It is interesting to note that the electronic dashboards, together with their voice synthesised warning announcement system were very short lived, returning quickly to the clearer analogue type instruments. The electronics had for some reason become even more complicated and brash than those previously fitted to the Maestro and many potential buyers of the Montego were pleased to find that conventional analogue instruments were again to be available at the latter end of 1984.

As a top of the range car there were special features only to be found on the MG Montego, which included a deeper front spoiler, along with a boot mounted one. Special cast alloy Dunlop TD type wheels were employed which enabled special low profile tyres to be fitted. In the event of a puncture or blow out at speed, the tyre would safely stay on the rim, allowing the car to be brought to a halt with no loss of control. Following on from its MG forerunners, the interior had a distinctive red bias with trim, carpeting, seat belts and piping all colour keyed. There was also central locking and

electrically operated front windows together with a quality four speaker stereo radio and cassette system all fitted as standard. These refinements all combined to make the MG Montego a very comfortable high speed up-market sports saloon, initially priced at over £8,000 it was to prove the fastest and most expensive production MG until upstaged by the ultra high performance MG Montego Turbo which was announced in April 1985. There were only cosmetic changes latterly to the MG Montego Efi similarly carried out on the MG Maestro. This consisted of dropping the Efi designation to be renamed the MG Montego 2.0i and likewise MG Maestro 2.0i. There were changes to the interior design, with slightly revised dashboard switching and the herringbone grey seating cloth was replaced with plain grey. The striking use of red piping and MG motifs continued, but gone was the bright red carpeting to be replaced by a more sober grey. A better quality 4 speaker sound system and a tilt and slide glass sunroof, with built-in sliding shade completed the interior facelift. Exterior wise, the alloy wheels were changed to a cross spoke design, whilst the only other visible changes amounted to colour-keyed door mirrors, discreet 2.0i badging on the rear bootlid and a smaller MG motif repositioned from the front grille to the leading edge of the bonnet. The British Racing Green MG Montego 2.0i featured is owned by David Wilks.

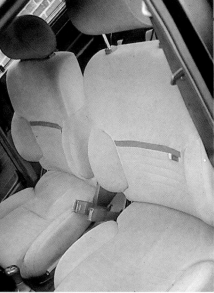

SPECIFICATION

Engine: 'O' series
No of cylinders: 4
Capacity: 1944 cc
Bore & Stroke: 84.5 mm x 89.0 mm
Valve gear: Overhead Camshaft
Fuel system: Lucas Electronic L type multi-point injection
Power Output: 115 bhp @ 5,500 rpm
Performance: 0-60 mph; 8.9 secs
Clutch: Dry plate
Gearbox: 5 speed all-synchromesh
Suspension: Independent front, semi-independent rear with coil springs
Wheels: Alloy, bolt-on
Brakes: Servo assisted, ventilated disc front, drums at rear
Wheelbase: 8' 5.2"
Track: front; 4' 10.5". Rear; 4' 9.8"

Montego Turbo Saloon

The closure of the MG factory at Abingdon also marked the end of production of the two seater sports cars that had been the hallmark for many years. Although the future of MG at that stage was quite uncertain, rumours abounded that the MG name was to be put on BL's new car the Metro, due to be announced on the 8th October 1980. The Metro originally appeared in standard form and it was not until May 1982, some 18 months after the Abingdon closure, that the MG Metro was announced with Sir Michael Edwardes saying, "The MG name is now proudly back on a BL product, and happily the MG Metro has been accepted by fiercely loyal MG enthusiasts as being in the MG tradition." The MG version of the Metro was quite widely acclaimed by the motoring press and the public alike and it was this car that was to set the scene for saloon based MGs that were to follow.

There were no recorded complaints that the MG Metro lacked performance, but very soon after the introduction of the car, just five months in fact, a turbocharged MG Metro was announced which was quite an exciting package, but at a price some people thought expensive. The car was priced at £5650 including tax which was some 17% more than the standard car, but the innovative installation of the turbo with electronic control gave smooth transition to turbo boost with plenty of top end power and it gave the feel of a car with a far larger engine than its modest 1275 cc. Following the Turbo there was a lot of speculation about a car codenamed LM 10 and this was to be the long awaited 5 door hatchback Maestro range. This was the first series of cars to make full use of Computer Aided Design (CAD for short) and Computer Aided Manufacture (CAM for short). All the car's exterior panels were defined by computer at the design stage and then transferred to computer controlled manufacture of the pressed steel panels. Crash tests were simulated by computer as well to determine such things as the gauge of the body panels and seat belt mounting points. The Maestro was to be built at a new high technology assembly plant at Cowley near Oxford and was assembled in the main by computer controlled robot arms, that carried out the work to very fine tolerances.

The MG version of the Maestro was introduced straightaway at the model launch and it was intended to be the flagship of the range although it did not differ greatly from others in the range. The car was considered by many, including the motoring press to be somewhat underdeveloped and rushed in order to meet the launch deadline of March 1983. Cosmetically the car was different, but the suspension, steering and brakes were no different to those on the standard models. Alloy wheels with Pirelli P8 tyres completed the package. The R series 1598 cc engine had minor modifications to the porting and the addition of twin 40 DCNF Weber carburettors on an 8 port manifold, thus raising the bhp from 81 on the standard 1600 unit to 103 bhp on the MG version. The choice of Weber carburettors proved wrong as the early production cars were plagued with hot starting problems due to fuel evaporation and after several factory post production modifications were fitted, it was possible to get the car to perform smoothly. An innovation on the MG Maestro was the introduction of computer LCD instrumentation, which some thought rather gimmicky and irritating, this being further developed and introduced on the

MG version of the LM 11 car, launched in April 1984 as the Montego. It is interesting to note that the electronic dashboards together with their voice synthesised warning announcement system were very short lived.

The Montego was to use the existing floorpan of the Maestro but was wider by 2" in the wheelbase, this provided more legroom for the rear seat passengers. Over 60% of the panels were the same as the Maestro, but the Montego was strictly a four door saloon and was considerably bigger being nearly 16" longer than the Maestro. The boot area was cavernous with 18.4 cu ft of space and the rear seat could fold down to accommodate long or bulky items. The MG Montego sported a version of the 'O' series engine which was originally intended for the MGB but only appeared in a few prototype models. This 2 litre engine was fitted with a new alloy cylinder head in which the inlet ports were paired together rather than alternated with the exhaust ports. The drive was through an all new Honda 5 speed gearbox to the front wheels. An electronic ignition system, together with Lucas L type electronic fuel injection gave 115 bhp @ 5500 rpm as opposed to 102 bhp on the normally aspirated engine. The electronic dashboard was a standard feature and had become even more complicated and brash than the one previously fitted to the Maestro, many potential buyers of the Montego were pleased to find that conventional analogue instruments were to be reverted to, at the latter end of 1984.

Features to be found only on the MG Montego, included a deeper front spoiler, along with a boot mounted one. Special cast alloy TD type wheels were employed which enabled low profile tyres to be fitted, which in the event of a puncture or blow out at speed would stay on the rim, allowing the car to be brought safely to a halt. Following on from its MG predecessors the interior had a distinctive red bias with trim, carpeting, seat belts and piping all colour keyed. There was also electrically operated central locking and front windows together with a four speaker stereo radio and cassette system. This all combined to make the MG Montego a very comfortable high speed upmarket sports saloon, initially priced at over £8,000 it was to become the most expensive production MG so far. The MG Maestro in the meantime was to see the introduction of the S series engine replacing the R series unit, this too was short lived in the 1600 version, confirming the suspicions that the original development of the Maestro was a rather hurried affair and was best forgotten about. The replacement for the 1600 MG Maestro was

announced in October 1984 and was altogether a better car. The MG Maestro Efi as it was to become known, utilised the 2 litre 'O' series fuel injected engine from the MG Montego and was greeted with enthusiasm, being an extremely quick car with an 0-60 time of 8.5 seconds.

Announced at the beginning of April 1985 was 'The fastest production MG ever made' the MG Montego Turbo with a top speed of 126 miles per hour and a 0-60 mph time of 7.3 seconds, quite startling performance for a 2 litre saloon. The 'O' series turbocharged engine produced 150 bhp @ 5,100 rpm and this was achieved through the Garrett AiResearch T3 turbocharger with a maximum boost pressure of 10 psi and an air to air intercooler fitted between the air cleaner and carburettor. The turbocharger was controlled by means of an integrated wastegate whose control system sensed turbocharger compressor discharge pressure. Engine intake manifold pressure was controlled to the desired levels by bypassing exhaust gas around the turbine and was the most efficient and practical method of control in terms of overall engine performance. As with the Efi MG Montego, the Lucas engine management system included programmed ignition and cylinder knock sensors. The single SU HIF44 carburettor was mounted at 35 degrees to the vertical with a unique inlet manifold with short inlet tracts to promote improved turbo response. An automatic choke was used utilising a stepper motor and fuel was supplied to the carburettor via a Bosch high pressure fuel pump delivering 40 psi. A regulator maintained the necessary pressure differential between the float valve and jet and was regulated so that it was always 5 psi above the air boost pressure. The plenum and carburettor were kept at a fairly constant temperature by means of a special thermostatically controlled cooling fan, ducting cool air to the carburettor. This avoided fuel evaporation and ensured smooth running and good throttle response under varying conditions. Heat dissipation was assisted by sodium filled stellite faced valves and the previously mentioned intercooler.

The 1994 cc engine produced 169 lb/ft of torque @ 3500 rpm and the power was transferred to the roadwheels via a Honda 5 speed close ratio gearbox. Suspension was uprated from the standard Efi Montego to obtain optimum handling balance whilst retaining good ride quality. The front and rear spring rate was increased and a thicker 22mm front anti-roll bar fitted together with the addition of a rear anti-roll bar. Front and rear dampers were pressurised gas filled units. The brakes were also uprated to 241 mm ventilated disc at the front with 203 mm rear drums and had servo assistance. They were fed by a dual circuit, diagonally split for safety. TD type alloy road wheels were fitted with HR rated 190/65-365 low profile tyres. A combination of front and rear spoilers brought down the drag coefficient (Cd) to 0.35 which also gave good stability at speed. Power assisted steering was standard and a heavy gauge torsion bar was fitted within the rack housing to give the required steering characteristics. Other standard features on the car were a tilt and slide steel sunroof, a four speaker stereo radio cassette system, electrically controlled and heated rear view mirrors and central door locking. As a top of the range car and taking account of the ehilarating performance, the Montego Turbo was considered very competitively priced.

MONTEGO TURBO

Specification:

Engine: Cast iron block with alloy head.
No of cylinders: 4 in line.
Capacity: 1994cc
Bore: 8.0mm
Stroke: 89.00mm
Compression ratio: 8.5:1
Valve Gear: single overhead belt driven camshaft.
Carburation: Blow through single SU HIF44 (sealed).
Turbocharger: Garrett AiResearch T3 with intercooler.
Ignition: Lucas fully programmed electronic, microprocessor controlled.
Peak boost pressure: 10 psi
Max Power: 150 bhp @ 5100 rpm
Max Torque: 169 lb/ft @ 3500 rpm
Transmission: 5 speed manual Honda close ratio.
Road wheels: Alloy TD rim 135 x 365 mm
Tyres: 190/65 HR 365 TD
Brakes: Front – ventilated 241 mm disc
      Rear – self adjusting drum 203 mm
Steering: Power assisted rack and pinion. 2.3 turns lock to lock.
Suspension: Front – Macpherson strut with uprated springs. Gas filled dampers and 22mm anti-roll bar.
      Rear – Semi-independent trailing arms with H beam, coil springs and gas filled dampers. Rear 14mm anti-roll bar.
Length: 4468 mm
Width: 1710 mm
Height: 1420 mm
Performance: Max speed, 126 mph. 0-60 mph, 7.3 secs., 50-70 mph, 6.6 secs. Standing quarter mile, 15.7 secs. Fuel consumption, 43 mpg at 56 mph.
Price new January '87: £11,396.

Maestro Turbo Saloon

The limited production MG Maestro Turbo once carried the distinction of being the fastest production car to carry the MG badge, only to be surpassed in more recent times by the low volume RV8. There were no precise figures available, but a production run of anything between 500 and 850 has been variously quoted in the motoring press. First launched at the October 1988 Motor Show, it was introduced as the last derivative of the Maestro range, before production ceased in favour of the Rover 200 range. Straight line performance figures put the MG hatchback in the supercar league with the advertising campaign proclaiming this. One such advert proudly stated "Faster than a Ferrari, a Porsche, a Lamborghini, a Lotus, an Aston.. " Maestro MG Turbo, 0-60, 6.7 secs. Certainly this was blistering performance and with a maximum speed of 130 mph the car set new standards for the modern sports saloons. The Turbo shared the same 'O' series engine as the 2.0i but in place of the fuel injection system a Garrett T3 Turbocharger with intercooler delivered fuel through a single variable choke SU carburettor at boost pressures up to 10 psi. The modified alloy cylinder head sported sodium filled valves to aid heat dissipation. Power was now enhanced from a standard 115 bhp on the 2.0i to 152 bhp on the Turbo and with an impressive torque figure

of 169 lb/ft @ 3,500 rpm to match, a lot of raw power was in reserve. Tickford Coachbuilders were charged with transforming the visual appearance of the Turbo which entailed the fitting of additional side skirts, deeper front and rear spoilers and an all enveloping tailgate spoiler. These body modifications along with the fitting of attractive spoked alloy wheels gave the car altogether a more aggressive look to compliment the performance.

The Maestro was originally launched in March 1983 and it was the first of a new generation of cars that were designed to revitalise the flagging corporate image of the Austin Rover Group and to take the company into the late 1980's in a far stronger market position. Built at a new high technology plant at Cowley near Oxford the LM10 (as it was codenamed) was the first of the Austin Rovers cars to make full. use of CAD/CAM (computer aided design/computer aided manufacture)technology. Huge investment surrounded the production of the new car and it put the company in the forefront of modern automated car design and computer controlled robot assembly. Additional use of the computer facilities included simulated crash testing which gave good indications of the likely stresses and deformation of panels prior to full crash testing at MIRA.

There were seven models in the Maestro range when launched and it was the MG version that was to be the flagship of the range. Only two power units were utilised in the complete range. The trusty 'A' series 1275 cc engine was augmented with the all new 'R' series engine of 1,598 cc which was of distant Maxi parentage. The MG Maestro 1600 was to have a special version of this power

unit and carried a single overhead camshaft and two twin choke downdraught 40 DCNF Weber Carburettors, these coupled to a special low loss inlet manifold boosted output from a standard 81 bhp to a respectable 103 bhp @ 6,000 rpm. The brief to the engineers was to have a high performance engine that was both smooth and tractable as well as making the car exciting to drive. Unfortunately the car was not particularly well received by both the motoring press and new owners due to bad carburation problems. It was felt that the MG 1600 had been rushed to

meet the launch date and consequently was underdeveloped. The principle problems centred around the Weber setup which did not seem entirely suited to the crossflow cylinder head. This caused very poor hot starting problems and many journalists felt that the car "ran out of steam above 6,000 rpm". The Weber version MG was very quickly replaced with the car now being powered by the 'S' series engine borrowed from the new Montego range. This unit differed from the earlier 'R' series engine in as much as it had a lighter and thinner walled cylinder block, an improved balanced crankshaft, a toothed drive for the camshaft, improved distributor drive, new oil pump and water pump and a redesigned cylinder head. This hasty change of power unit simply confirmed the earlier fears that the car had been too rapidly developed and it was when only 3,000 units bearing this 'S' series engine had been produced that yet again there was another change of engine, but at this time the opportunity was taken to implement a few cosmetic changes as well.

The new MG Maestro Efi was announced in October 1984 and was altogether a far better car than its predecessors. Employing a two litre fuel injected 'O' series engine this power unit had the benefit of fully programmed ignition with knock sensing and the Lucas 'L' type multi-point fuel injection system. A brand new close-ratio 5 speed Honda gearbox transferred the power, now quoted at 115 bhp, to the front wheels. Performance was now fairly brisk with a 0-60 mph time of 8.5 secs and to cater for this increased performance, the front brakes were uprated to the ventilated type and tyres were changed from SR rating to HR specification. The Efi MG remained as a Maestro option right through to the end of Maestro production when it was phased out along with all the other variants in favour of the new Rover 200 series. Latterly the MG version was designated the MG 2.0i and this car was available alongside the MG Maestro Turbo before these cars took their place in the MG history books along with the MG Metro and MG Montego performance saloons towards the end of 1981. The featured car belongs to Andy Bradley.

MAESTRO TURBO

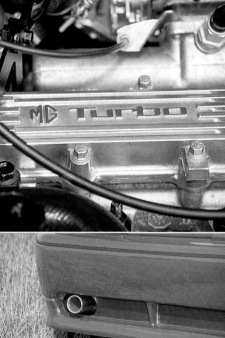

SPECIFICATION

Engine
No of cylinders: 4 in line
Capacity: 1,994 cc
Bore & Stroke: 84.5 mm x 89 mm
Valve operation: Single ohc, two valves per cyl
Fuel system: Garret T3 turbo through single SU
Max Power: 150 bhp @ 5,100 rpm
Max Torque: 169 lb/ft @ 3,500 rpm
Transmission
Type: 5 speed manual
Suspension
Front: Independent McPherson strut, lower
wishbones, coil springs, anti roll bar
Rear: Semi independent torsion beam axle, trailing
arms, coil springs, anti roll bar
Brakes: Disc front, drum rear with servo assistance
Steering: Rack and pinion, power assisted
Wheels: 5J x 15. Tyres: 185/55 R15
Performance
0-60 mph; 6.7 secs
Max Speed: 132 mph
Fuel comsumption: 22.2 mpg
Price new 1989: £13,529

MG RV8

After years of rumour, gossip and speculation Rover finally put an MG back on their production menu in 1992. Before the truth came out, it was feared that another hatchback badged with an MG logo may be on offer. To Rover's eternal credit they produced a wind-in-the-hair, sleek lined new sportscar worthy of this Heritage steeped marque. The launch to the world was at the Motor Show on 20th October 1992 and at the show, Rover's Director of Special Projects Steve Schlemmer who was responsible for the RV8 from inception to finish explained just why 1992 was the year chosen for the launch: "Two years ago I was given the task to assess the initial feasibility of the project and to discover and satisfy specific customer needs. The idea had actually existed since the late 1980's when Heritage's MGB bodyshell brought our attention to the still massive popularity of the car. BMIHT thought it impractical and inappropriate to remake the MGB again as a whole car, so we branched towards a different track. "Obviously, Rover manufacture cars to make money, not nostalgia. We needed a 'hook to hang it on; a symposium gave us the decision to follow it through its evolution to the Nineties. Celebrating its thirtieth birthday seemed the ideal 'hook' and judging from the enthusiastic response we have received already, we appear to have made the right decision."
Extensive customer research was carried out prior to design "so we could aim the car at its ideal market" continued Steve. "We interviewed relatively well-off, two/three car families with owners interested in owning a classic but worried about maintenance and reliability; most wanted a 'toy' for Sundays rather than a vehicle for primary transport. We realised that we didn't have to compete with other state of the art 1993 sports cars and veered instead towards a progressive car but still retaining MG charisma."
The result was clear for all to see, although heavily reliant on the MGB, the RV8 was a desirable, top of the range sportscar very much of the Nineties yet distinctively resembling the timeless MGB. Curvaceous lines surrounded a powerful 3.9 litre fuel injected engine, perceived outwardly by the tell tale bonnet bulge, a power output of 188 bhp made it by far the quickest MG ever produced. Based on the MGB bodyshell, the RV8 was hand built by Rover at its Cowley factory in Oxford. The estimated breakdown of components used in the project was approximately 5% actual MGB parts, 20% derived therefrom and 75% completely new. Viewed from the exterior, the changes compared to the MGB included fully integrated front and rear bumpers finished in the same body colour with recessed fog lights; the headlamps were sloping instead of the vertical lenses of the MGB and the original two piece grille was replaced by a one piece unit with the famous Octagon badge, reverting back to the days of brown and cream, dropped neatly into the front grille. The windscreen was modified into a single unit, making replacement easier and better aerodynamically. Gone were the quarterlights, instead a one piece side door glass naturally added extra security. Overall, the car appeared more rounded and squat, achieved through widening the front and rear track and the slightly flaring the wheel arches achieved a wider image and deeper moulded bumpers front and rear completed the very pleasing body treatment.
The hood was designed in conjunction with

Tickford and based on the original frame, it now featured a zip-out backlight designed to prevent creasing. It was claimed that the whole unit was very easy to raise and lower, being retained by two simple 'over-centre' catches on the windscreen header rail. The interior was a sumptuous concoction of light coloured stone beige leather and Burr Elm veneer, whilst the instrument panel was carried over from the MGB however the instrumentation was all new. A rev counter and speedometer flanked the fuel gauge behind the steering wheel whilst to the right were front and rear fog lamps and hazard warning light switches, all in traditional analogue style. The centre console housed a clock, temperature and battery condition instruments along with heater and radio cassette. Lighting indicators and wipers were fitted on the steering column, ending in a leather covered three spoke steering wheel. The seats were well padded and very comfortable giving the impression of a higher driving position than on the old MGB. Chrome door pulls and chrome window winders interrupted the flow of leather. The luxury beige carpeting was moulded in a continuous piece for improved sound deadening and fit.
Housed under the sleek exterior of the RV8 was the powerful 3.9 litre Rover V8 engine producing 190 PS (around 188 bhp). The electronic fuel injection and two threeway closed-loop catalysts returned blistering performance with excellent midrange acceleration. The transmission utilised the Rover 77mm 5 speed gearbox, which had an excellent record of durability being paired with the V8 engine for many years with success. A Quaiffe torque-sensing differential was fitted as standard, originally developed for rally cars it offered smooth and consistent performance with optimum torque transfer characteristics. Traction was transferred from the slipping wheel to the wheel with grip automatically. Utilising a series of spiral gears reacting against the differential casing, harshness and snatch were eliminated.
Rover concentrated on safe and predictable handling for the RV8 when designing the chassis package and reported a superior ride qual-

ity over the original MGB. The front suspension utilised a double wishbone layout with coil springs and concentric Koni dampers. The assembly was mounted on a modified version of the original MGB front crossmember which carried all the suspension loads and on which was mounted the steering rack. Front swivel hub and stub axle assemblies were new, with conventional 'sealed for life' ball joints for the upper mountings. Goldline spherical bearings, as used on Formula 1, formed the lower mountings. Rear suspension was based on the original but telescopic Koni dampers replacing the old hydraulic lever arm systems. A 'torque bias' differential controlled the performance potential of the RV8 and the axle location was improved by the addition of twin lower torque control arms. Ride and handling were improved due to the low friction, twin taper-leaf design rear springs. Anti roll bars were fitted front and rear as standard.
The brakes were a dual circuit, servo assisted system, featuring 272mm diameter ventilated front discs with four pot calipers and 9" rear drums. Smart alloy road wheels of lattice spoke design complemented the car whilst the wheel nuts were fully covered by a hexagonal wheel centre cap, undone only with the aid of a key for security reasons. Six standard body colours were available: Flame Red, White Gold Metallic, Black, British Racing Green, Nightfire Red Pearlescent and Caribbean Blue Pearlescent. In addition, four other colours special only to the RV8 (at extra cost) could be obtained: Le Mans Green Metallic, Woodcote Green, Oxford Blue Pearlescent and Old English White.
Although not running as a true 'limited edition' the RV8 commenced production in Spring 1993 at the build rate of approximately 15 per week. It was planned that production would run for 18 to 24 months at least, culminating in a total build of approximately 2,000 cars. Although at the time Rover would divulge no further secrets as to future MG plans, the RV8 was seen as a very worthy "stop gap" to keep the MG name to the forefront whilst the all-new MG project codenamed PR3 was under development.

MG RV8

SPECIFICATION

Engine: Rover V8
Capacity: 3,950 cc
No of cylinders: 8 in 90 degree vee formation
Bore: 94mm
Stroke: 71.12mm
Compression ratio: 9.35:1
Valve gear: Single camshaft, 2 valves per cylinder
Fuel system: Lucas multi-point injection
Max Power: 190 ps @ 4,750 rpm
Max Torque: 318 mm @ 3,200 rpm
Performance: 0-60 mph 5.9 secs
Max Speed: 135 mph
Transmission: Rover LT77, 5 speed manual gearbox
Suspension: front; Independent, double wishbone, coil springs and telescopic dampers with anti-roll bar rear; Live axle with twin taper leaf half elliptic springs and telescopic dampers. Twin lower torque control arms with anti-roll bar
Steering: Rack and pinion
Brakes: front; 270mm ventilated discs. Rear; 9" drums with servo assistance
Wheels: Cast spoked alloy
Rim width: 15" x 6J
Tyres: 205/65 x VR15
Fuel Capacity: 51 litres
Fuel grade: Unleaded 95 RON
Weight: Gross vehicle weight 1280 Kg
Dimensions: Wheelbase; 2330 mm
         Length; 4010 mm
         Track front; 1260 mm. rear; 1330 mm
         Height; 1320 mm
         Width; 1694 mm
Price: £26,500

MGF 1.8i & 1.8i VVC

Almost seventy years since "Old Number One" was built in the MG Car Company's factory, in Edmund Road, Oxford the first "all new" MG model to be produced for 33 years was launched by Rover Group at the Geneva Motor Show on March 7th 1995. The MGF follows in the true tradition of the marque and is an exceptionally stylish and refined two seater sports car that will carry the famous octagon badge through well into the next century. Many mourned the closure of the MG factory in Abingdon in 1980, but economics dictated that with no new sports models in the pipeline and declining sales of the MGB and Midget models, a decision was taken to pull out from sports car manufacture and concentrate on mainstream volume car production. In 15 years there have been many changes in the fortunes of the Rover Group with the Company now enjoying an enhanced image and record

breaking sales of its volume cars. This turnaround and latterly the acquisition of the Rover Group by BMW has ensured the fruition of project "Phoenix" or PR3 to give it the correct codename. The project first started in 1989 and followed on from the concept car MG EX-E upon which the PR3 is very loosely based. This was unveiled at the Frankfurt Motor Show in 1985 and received exceptional press acclaim, unfortunately EX-E was only to be a design exercise but it definitely set the scene for the eventual launch of the MGF which carries overtones of the EX-E particularly in its rear-end styling.

The MGF is produced in two versions with the base model designated the 1.8i and the higher specification model known as the 1.8i VVC. Much emphasis has been put on safety with the MGF offering exceptional standards of handling coupled with agility. This is achieved with a mid engine configuration driving the rear wheels. Suspension is of the double wishbone type with servo assisted disc brakes both front and rear. ABS is available as an option on the base model and fitted as standard on the 1.8i VVC. Power steering is introduced for the first time on an MG sports car and highly sophisticated it is too. The system is computer controlled and speed sensitive, introducing more assistance at manoeuvring speed. This does not mean that the steering lacks any "feel" in fact it has allowed the engineers to produce a very positive and responsive system with a very high lock to lock ratio. The electric power unit has self diagnostics built in and a fail safe device which will allow unassisted steering in the event of any failure and weighs a considerable 5 kg less than conventional power

steering units. Another advantage with this type of electronic unit is the fact that there is no perceptible noise from the unit, unlike the hydraulic systems that normally "hiss and groan" at manoeuvering speed. The provision of power assistance also contributes greatly to improved fuel economy and emissions.

The 1796 cc fuel injected power units in both variants are the award winning Rover 'K' series engines mounted transversally. Great importance has been placed providing high levels of performance coupled with excellent fuel economy and very low servicing costs combined with a very moderately priced replacement parts policy. The base model MGF has a power output of 120 PS @ 5,500 rpm with a 0-60 mph time of 8.5 seconds and a top speed of 120 mph, whilst the 1.8i VVC model has a unique Variable Valve Control (VVC) system that achieves 145 PS @ 7,000 rpm with a 0-60 mph time of 7.0 seconds and a top speed of 130 mph. A three way catalytic loop ensure that the engine emissions comply with and exceed the ECD regulations set for introduction in January 1997.

There is no mistaking that this ultra modern sports car is an MG with subtle reminders of the heritage and tradition of the marque. From the front there are hints of MGB from the rear there are the aforementioned traces of the EX-E prototype and as you would expect the famous octagon badge is to be found on many parts of the car. Overall the MGF has very sleek modern styling which is well balanced and pleasing to the eye when viewed from any angle. The design and manufacture of the body shell are the result of collaboration between Rover and the Coventry-based Motor Panels Plc which is part of the Mayflower Group. A stylish hardtop secured by four clips compliments the car, but only comes painted gloss black. The interior of the MGF is tastefully appointed with all controls and the comprehensive instrumentation well placed. The cream instrument dials and leather trimmed steering wheel (on 1.8i VVC only) are in keeping with the MG heritage, whilst modern refinements include electric windows, computer controlled seat belt pre-tensioners and a top of the range audio system. Seating is very comfortable and supportive, whilst maintaining a stylish appearance and is cloth covered on the base model but black leather with cloth inserts on the VVC version.

An area which has received a great deal of attention from designers and engineers is the safety aspect. The MGF has one of the

strongest bodies ever constructed for this type of vehicle. Side impact beams are integrated into the door construction and provide the occupants with a very high level of protection. This protection is further enhanced by reinforced waistline rails and in the event of a roll-over situation the sturdy windscreen frame conceals high tensile roll-over tubes. Occupants also have the benefit of airbags, which come as standard for the driver and an option for the passenger. Security also majored on the list of priorities when the car was at the design stage. The MGF boast and extensive anti-theft system which consists of superlocking for the doors and boot, coupled with passive engine immobilisation. The alarm monitors both volumetrically and perimetrically and affords protection to the car even with the hood down. A sensible innovation from the security aspect on an open topped car is the fact that the bonnet pull is secured in the lockable boot. The distinctive alloy wheels have built in security locks.

The MGF has been produced to compliment Rovers' already very successful range of vehicles and in keeping with that existing range has extremely high levels of build quality and reliability. The MGF will not be built in such high volumes as Rovers' mainstream models, but the European sportscar niche market is where the MGF is fairly and squarely aimed. It was important that the car should be affordable in the true tradition of MG and the 1.8i and 1.8i VVC are priced around £15,500 and £18,000 respectively. Cost of ownership was another major consideration in the planning of the car and features that have been incorporated in the MGF reflect this commitment to keep running costs down. Such features as easy panel replacement, clip on headlamp lenses (negating the need to replace the whole light unit in event of stone breakage), retracting indicator lenses absorbing low speed nudges (to avoid breakage), easily replaceable soft top rear window, Long life spark plugs that only require changing every 66,000 miles, and 12,000 mile service intervals all contribute to keeping running costs down and are claimed by Rover to be 50% of an equivalent competitors model. A comprehensive range of accessories is available for the MGF, ranging from fully integrated luggage through to child seats and cycle carriers. To cater for the European buyers, snow chains and ski racks are a welcome choice.

The MGF will be sold by a network of approximately 120 specialised Rover dealers in the UK that have been specifically selected and trained to give the best possible levels and support that a car such as the MGF demands. Continental Europe and Japan are other markets which are key targets although the MGF is not destined for the North American market which was so successful for the TC, TD, TF, MGA, MGB and Midget.

MGF 1.8i & 1.8iVVC

1.8i

1.8i VVC

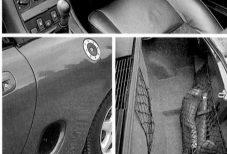

1.8i VVC

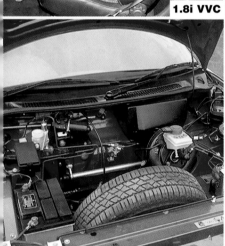

1.8i

1.8i VVC

SPECIFICATION
MGF

- Two seater sports car of unitary steel construction.
- Soft top. (Hard top available as an option)
- Mid engine, transverse mounted, rear wheel drive.
- Two models available with different versions of the 1.8 litre Rover 'K' series engine.

1.8i   K series 1796 cc 16 valve
      Power: 120 PS @ 5,500 rpm
      Torque: 166 Nm @ 3,000 rpm

1.8i VVC   K series 1796 cc 16 valve with Variable Valve Control (VVC)
      Power: 145 PS (110 Kw) @ 7,000 rpm
      Torque: 174 Nm @ 4,400 rpm

- 5 speed manual transmission.
- Independent suspension all round with double wishbones and Hydragas springs, interconnected front to rear. Front and rear anti-roll bars fitted as standard.
- 4 wheel disc brakes with ABS optional on the 1.8i derivative, standard on the 1.8i VVC.
- Speed sensitive (electric) power assisted steering.
- 15" alloy road wheels with 6J rims, 185/55 x VR15 tyres.

Dimensions and weight

Length	3913 mm
Width	1628 mm
Height (hood up)	1264 mm
Wheelbase	2375 mm
Track (front & rear)	1394 mm
Weight	1055 Kg (1.8i)
	1065 Kg (1.8i VVC)
Cd	0.36

Performance Maximum speed:
1.8i: 120 mph   **1.8i VVC:** 130 mph
0-60 mph: **1.8i:**   8.5 seconds
          1.8i VVC: 7.0 seconds

Acknowledgements

My sincere thanks are due to the owners of the fine MGs portrayed within this book. Their patience is to be recognised whilst they spent seemingly endless time manoeuvring their car into position for the desired picture. Their help with the location of suitable venues for the photographs is also much appreciated. I am indebted to them for their help with information on the history of the vehicles and the loan of original brochures and period photographs is also acknowledged. Since the project started in *Enjoying MG* in January 1985, I am aware that some of the MGs featured have changed ownership, nonetheless, I would like to thank the following members of the MG Owners' Club, MG Car Club and MG Octagon Car Club for their help, for without their willing co-operation there would be no book.

Tony Newbold, Chris Cridland, Dave Keen, David Bryant, Malcolm Green, Tony Stafford, Richard Taylor, Phil Jones, Ted Waters, Malcolm Badger, Eric Nicholls, Clive and Chris Postles, Derek Baker and Richard Hutton, Rod Dunnett, Ray Shrubb, Graham Paddy, Maureen Sawyer, Keith Pomeroy, Neil Reynolds, Jon Ridley, Nick Atkins, Tim Hodgkinson, Dave Jarvis, Kim Baker, Peter Morgan, John & Pam Hall, Geoff Radford, Bill Donaldson, Cathy Barton, Susie Shenston, Mark Durocher-Weston, Dave Ransome, David Wilks and Andy Bradley.

I must also record my appreciation to Kevin Jones of Rover Group for his assistance with the photographing of the Metro 6R4 rally car and the new MGF sports car.

Bibliography

The following books were used as a source of reference:

MG by McComb, by Wilson McComb
The MG Story, by Anders Ditlev Clausager
Magic of MG, by Mike Allison
Magic of the Marque, by Mike Allison
The Art of Abingdon, by John McLellan
MG Sports Car, by Autocar
Great Marques, by Chris Harvey
Autocar (formerly *The Autocar*)
Dream Machines, by Ian Penberthy
Original T Series, by Anders Ditlev Clausager
The Mighty MGs, by Graham Robson
The MGA, MGB and MGC, by Graham Robson